UNLESS HASTE IS MADE
there will be none left
at the Sandwich Islands to civilize,
except the civilizers themselves.
Théodore-Adolphe Barrot

The Monument Raised in Hawaii to Captain Cook

Fisquet

UNLESS HASTE IS MADE

A FRENCH SKEPTIC'S ACCOUNT OF THE SANDWICH ISLANDS IN 1836

Théodore-Adolphe Barrot

Translated by Rev. Daniel Dole

Illustrated By
Barthelme Lauvergne & Théodore Auguste Fisquet

Introduction by Arthur Nagasawa

PRESS PACIFICA * KAILUA * HAWAII

Library of Congress Cataloging in Publication Data

Barrot, Theodore Adolphe, 1803-1870.
    Unless haste is made.

    Translation of Les Iles Sandwich, which was originally
published in Revue des deux mondes, Aug. 1 and 15, 1839.
    Includes index.
    1. Hawaii—Description and travel—to 1950.
2. Barrot, Theodore Adolphe, 1803-1870. I. Title.
DU623.B32213   919.69'04'2   77-27597
ISBN 0-916630-05-6
ISBN 0-916630-04-8 pbk

The prints of Lauvergne and Fisquet are reproduced by permission of the
Hawaiian Historical Society.

FIRST TIME IN BOOK FORM

Manufactured by Edwards Brothers, Incorporated, Ann Arbor,
Michigan.

PRESS PACIFICA / P.O.BOX 47 / KAILUA, HI 96734

EDITOR'S PREFACE

Théodore-Adolphe Barrot was thirty-two years old when he arrived in Hawaii in 1836. Behind him lay a well-established career in the French diplomatic service. In fact, it was a change in diplomatic posts which brought about his visit to the Sandwich Islands, for Barrot was en route to the Philippines to assume the position of French consul there.

Barrot's writing shows him to have been very much a man of his time. Like countless other Europeans, Barrot had read the journals of Captain James Cook whose discovery of the Sandwich Isles catapulted the isolated island chain into international fame. One of Barrot's primary interests was estimating the effects of Western civilization on the islanders.

In his assessment, Barrot takes us back to that period in history when Europeans tended to think of all primitive peoples as more natural than, and therefore superior to, the "corrupted" citizens of urbanized societies. It is in this context that Barrot used the term "savage" throughout his account. The "noble savage" of late eighteenth and early nineteenth century literature was clearly in Barrot's thoughts when he wrote,

"We were disappointed, for these were not the islanders of Cook, and although the influence of the savage state still bore sway in the physical and moral constitution of each individual, it was no longer that of simple and guileless nature, which we were expecting to study. Yet, in the first part of our intercourse with them we were the best able to discover the traces of what the Sandwich Islands were, at the time of their discovery; later, we found the villages more European, and the people almost as vicious as those who have civilized them."

Travelling from villages to palaces, Barrot's diplomatic status served him well. King Kamehameha III received him cordially and granted several audiences to Barrot, both in his palace and at the home of his sister, Nahienaena. It is here that we get a glimpse of the tragic young woman who would die within two months. "When informed that she was only twenty years of age, I was surprised," Barrot recorded, "she seemed to me much older." The diplomat discreetly avoided any reference to the incestuous relationship between the king and Nahienaena. Perhaps he sensed that European readers would not be able to understand the sacredness of such a relationship in the ancient customs of Hawaii.

Barrot originally published his work in two installments in *Revue des Deux Mondes* (Paris, 1839) under the title, "Les Iles Sandwich." In 1845, the Rev. William Richards brought a copy of Barrot's account to Hawaii on his return from a diplomatic mission in Europe. By 1850, the Rev. Daniel Dole had translated the article into English for publication in Hawaii. Entitled "Visit of the French Sloop of War *Bonite,* to the Sandwich Islands, in 1836," it appeared serially in *The Friend* from January to November, 1850.

When the articles reached the public, concern over French intervention in Hawaii was running high. In August, 1849, French war ships had threatened to lay siege to Honolulu over supposed insults to the French consul. In addition, the general question of land ownership which Barrot addresses at some length had, by 1850, focused to an emotional political issue. Barrot's article, written fourteen years earlier, had suddenly become timely.

Now, one hundred twenty-seven years later, Dole's translation of Barrot's account reappears in this volume. Some silent corrections in punctuation have been made, and where noted (†), a few awkward renderings have been eased into clearer English. A new title, taken from Barrot's own words, has been added to this edition, the first in book form.

A few words should be written about the illustrations. Travelling with Barrot were two artists, Barthelme Lauvergne and Théodore Auguste Fisquet, members of the French scientific expedition aboard the *Bonite.* The artists provided not only botanical illustrations for the scientists but recorded events of the journey as well. Their drawings originally appeared in *Voyage Autour du Monde...1836 et 1837...Album Historique* (Paris, c. 1841). Tantalizing evidence in Barrot's account indicates that sketches were made of members of the royal court, including Kinau, Kekauluohi, and Liliha. Despite careful search, the sketches could not be found. More happily, textual evidence also suggests that it is Kapiolani we see riding past the Captain Cook monument. Although the figure is distant, it may be the only likeness of Kapiolani in existence.

We would like to express our appreciation to those whose help has made the publication of this volume possible. Mary Jane Knight, Hawaii Mission Children's Society Library, first directed our attention to M. Barrot's work, and Barbara Dunn, librarian for the Hawaiian Historical Society, provided access to the illustrations which appear in this edition. Elizabeth Larson, Hawaii Mission Children's Society Library, graciously provided answers to our most difficult questions. Ellen Chapman of Hamilton Library, University of Hawaii, managed to locate for us a copy of the elusive French text, and Eleanor B. Frierson advised us in resolving questions of translation. These and the librarians of Bishop Museum and the Hawaiiana and the Pacific collection, University of Hawaii, we thank for their interest and support.

Penny Pagliaro

INTRODUCTION

by

Arthur Nagasawa

The year 1819 was a crucial turning point in the history of the Hawaiian kingdom. Kamehameha I, the founder of the Hawaiian monarchy, died. In that same year the first New England missionaries set sail for Hawaii. In addition, the vanguard of unruly men in their whaling ships made their appearance in Hawaiian waters. As time went on, business and commercial interests followed, transforming the docile native kingdom into the ways of older societies.

Two forces eventually emerged as the leading competitors for the control of the Hawaiian kingdom: the American missionaries from New England, and commercial and business interests, largely American and British. During the first few decades after the reign of Kamehameha I, the missionaries came to wield the dominant influence over the Hawaiian king and his subjects.

What were the effects of these early competing influences on the native Hawaiians? How successful was the Hawaiian king in sustaining his sovereignty over the increasing power and influence of the missionaries? How effective was the native monarchial system in nurturing the general welfare of the common people, the *makaainana*? Did Protestant Christianity succeed in displacing the indigenous native religion and culture and in uplifting the Hawaiians? What were the causes of the decline in the native population? Were the goals espoused by the missionaries for the Hawaiian people appropriate for their needs?

The answers to these questions, as well as other affecting descriptions and observations, are presented by Théodore Barrot, a passenger on the French frigate *Bonite* which visited the Hawaiian Islands in 1836. An erudite observer with eclectic interests, Barrot probes and analyzes the conditions of the Hawaii of those years with a keen reportorial eye, introducing his readers to such personages as King Kamehameha III (Kauikeaouli), Kapiolani, Kinau, the *kuhina nui*, Don Marin, and Charlton, the British consul general.

Though the year 1836 was only a short seventeen years after the death of Kamehameha I and the first incursions of the missionaries, whalers, and other visitors, Hawaii was already in a transitional stage of development. The missionaries were definitely in control, imposing on the primitive native society a puritanical way of life common to the New England churchmen of those days.

Barrot concedes that the missionaries accomplished an important service by spreading Christianity among a people whose old religion had been destroyed. However, missionary opposition to foreign business ventures and foreign immigration which might lead to agricultural development seem to him as misguided as their imposition of an intolerant state religion. In Barrot's estimation, the missionaries' concentration on purely religious efforts and their failure to effect a material uplifting of the natives worked to the detriment of the Hawaiians.

Barrot urges the need to invite immigrants so that the industry and economy of the islands could be developed. He questions the value of Hawaiian policies which denied foreigners property rights. He points out the need to liberalize the Hawaiian government and the narrow goals of the missionary counselors so that business and commercial interests could provide the native commoners with an economic stake in society, thereby encouraging self-reliance and temporal well-being as a balance to purely religious ends.

Had Théodore Barrot sailed to the Hawaiian Islands in 1852, less than two decades later, he would have found a changed Hawaii, for the substance of his recommendations had been realized by that date. By mid-nineteenth century the native king and chiefs had surrendered their autocratic powers. A liberal constitution had been adopted, thus limiting the erstwhile power of the king and *aliis* over the commoners. Foreign populations in the Hawaiian kingdom enjoyed the franchise and were allowed to own land. Further, the influence of the missionaries was on the decline as business and commercial interests gained in wealth, power, the influence and moved the government toward the direction of the American ideal of separation of church and state.

At the same time, however, Barrot would have found that the native Hawaiians, many of whom were as yet untried in the ways of an advanced democratic system of self-government, were not able to help themselves through the liberalized system of government; nor were they able to compete with the aggressive land-hungry visitors in the open, competitive market. Under such circumstances the foreign community in Hawaii, welded together around a nexus of business and commercial interests, soon secured both political and economic ascendancy over Hawaii. The liberal land law of 1850 and the democratic constitution of 1852 were, ironically, the penultimate end for the native Hawaiians, for during the second half of the nineteenth century events moved swiftly toward the "revolution" of 1893.

Théodore Barrot laments the fact that France is falling behind the other powers in Hawaii. He attributes this situation to the policy of the Hawaiian monarchs, who were controlled by the fanatically religious regents, Kaahumanu and Kinau. The regents, in turn, were under missionary influence, a situation which kept the Americans in dominance by discouraging any French religious or economic participation. Barrot spoke as a patriotic French citizen whose home government was then involved in an expansionist competition in the Pacific basin. As such, his views of the American-dominated island kingdom could have been subjective. Nevertheless, for the serious reader, Théodore-Adolphe Barrot's *Unless Haste is Made: A French Skeptic's Account of the Sandwich Islands in 1836* adds another dimension to the interpretation of early Hawaiian history through his acute observations of conditions in the island kingdom in 1836.

Chaminade University of Honolulu

LIST OF ILLUSTRATIONS

TABLE OF CONTENTS

Running Aground in the Sandwich Islands

Lauvergne

CHAPTER ONE

Leaving Guayaquil, August 14th, 1836, we came in sight of Hawaii in the night of September 29th. From early morning we looked with impatience, in the direction where we supposed the island would appear. According to the accounts of navigators, we ought, at a great distance, to perceive Mauna Loa, the mysterious summit of which had not, for a long time, been visited by any European. It entered into our plans to explore its almost inaccessible gorges, to cross over the snows which crown it, and inscribe our names upon its most elevated peak; this for some days was the almost constant subject of our conversation. In vain the recital of the numerous accidents to which we should expose ourselves; in vain did they tell us of M. Douglas, an English naturalist, who had perished under the horns of a wild bull while engaged in a like enterprise; danger seemed to impart new attractions to our scientific expedition, and our eyes sought to distinguish, through the clouds, the theatre of our approaching explorations; but a thick curtain of vapors concealed it all day from our view. Yet this often happens; for the clouds, driven almost the whole year by the N.E. trade winds are obstructed in their passage by the wall formed by this group of islands and rest upon the summits of the mountains.

The night came, and, about an hour before day, the noise of the breakers announced to us that we were near land. We tacked about, and at day break, found ourselves ten or twelve leagues from the island of Hawaii. We saw Mauna Loa rising with an almost imperceptible ascent, and we were astonished, we even regretted not to find it more elevated. It will soon appear that we misjudged the difficulties which awaited us.

All day we were either becalmed, or the winds were so light that we were unable to approach the land; it was not until the next day, Oct. 1st, that we went on shore.

Yet the 29th of September did not pass without affording some satisfaction to our curiosity. When four or five leagues distant from land, we saw a canoe approaching, manned with four savages. The desire to see us must have been strong indeed to induce them to venture so far in so frail a craft. We preceived that they were naked, their heads wreathed with foliage. It was the first specimen of man in the savage state that most of us had ever seen; and our disappointment may be easily imagined when we perceived that instead of altering our course to approach them, we were passing them as if scarcely worth our notice. I pitied the poor creatures; the ship passed within a hundred fathoms of their canoe; they seemed astonished; they stopped a moment, wiping the sweat from their faces with the backs of their hands; then, as we receded we could see them making signs to us with their paddles; was it in token of friendship? or did they intend to reproach us? At length they turned their canoe towards the shore, upon which we discerned, by the aid of our spy-glasses, a number of huts in the midst of a grove of cocoa-nut trees.

The next day, our disappointment was more than made up. As we approached the land, an innumerable multitude of canoes put off towards us, and in less than an hour, the deck of the *Bonite* was covered with islanders. The first hesitated to come on board, but soon it was necessary to station sentinels at the ladders, in order to avoid a complete invasion. Almost all were naked, with the exception of a sort of girdle called *maro;* some, the aged principally, were tattooed; the names of many appeared, in large letters, on their arms or breasts. It was easy to perceive that they were beginning to be accustomed to the sight of Europeans. From their bargains we were assured that civilized men had been here: *tala tala* (dollar) was what they most generally asked of us. In exchange for shells, fowls, hogs &c., which they brought us, they were willing to take nothing but money, or clothing. And surely, to see the airs of importance which he arrogated to himself

among his companions, who found himself the for-
tunate owner of a watchcoat, a shirt, or any part of
European apparel, easily convinced us of the value
which they attached to such articles.

We were disappointed, for these were not the
islanders of Cook, and although the influence of the
savage state still bore sway in the physical and moral
constitution of each individual, it was no longer that of
simple and guileless nature, which we were expecting
to study. Yet, in the first part of our intercourse with
them we were the best able to discover the traces of
what the Sandwich Islands were, at the time of their
discovery: later, we found the villages more European;
and the people almost as vicious as those who have
civilized them.

A Portugese, who had lived on the island for a long
time, and whom it would have been somewhat difficult
to distinguish from a savage, served us as a pilot, and at
noon we were anchored in the bay of *Kealakeakua*.
More than 200 canoes were around the *Bonite*, yet
we had not seen a single woman. This surprised us;
for the accounts of divers voyagers had informed us that
no sooner was a vessel arrived than it was surrounded
by a crowd of women, veritable water-nymphs, who
dove and swam around, pointing to the land and making
known to the sailors, by their lascivious postures,
the pleasures to be enjoyed there; but the pilot soon
explained the mystery. "Ships," said he, "are *tabu*
to women; it is a law of the missionaries." He gave
us an account, at the same time, of several measures

taken by the missionaries for the promotion of morals and religion; but more of this hereafter.

The bay of Kealakeakua extends four or five leagues from North to South; the deepest part is a sort of cove formed by two points of low land projecting into the sea on the right and left. This cove is commanded by a mountain, or wall of blackish lava, four or five hundred feet in perpendicular height. On the left is the village of *Kaawaloa,* to the right, surrounded with cocoa-nut trees, we perceived the village of Kealakeakua, which has given name to the bay, and beyond, towards the extremity of the point, another village, the name of which I do not remember. Upon the high lands, which overlook the bay, we distinguished a number of houses, and among them, one which seemed built in the European style: "It is," said the pilot, "the house of the missionary Forbes; the village is called *Upper Kaawaloa."*

In the afternoon we went to Kaawaloa. We had some difficulty in landing; yet with the assistance of the Indians, many of whom plunged into the water to bring us aid, and after some falls upon the rocks, we found ourselves on terra firma. The village of Kaawaloa seemed to be composed of only about fifty houses. The bread-fruit and cocoa-nut trees give to it a picturesque appearance. A species of English sailor, steward of Kapiolani, chief of this district, came to inform us that his mistress was ready to receive us. We readily accepted the invitation of the noble lady, and we found her seated outside of the enclosure which surrounds her house, in the shade of a bread-fruit tree. She was about fifty years of age, of a colossal stature, five feet and eight or ten inches at least, very corpulent and very ugly. She received us politely. I hesitated a moment whether, according to what I had read in Cook's voyages, I should not salute her in the ancient manner of the country, by rubbing my nose against hers; I looked to see if some gesture would not show that this was her desire; but, not observing anything in her attitude which betokened the necessity of the Hawaiian salutation, I was satisfied with taking the hand which she offered me. Some seats, real European chairs, were brought us and we seated ourselves around Kapiolani. Behind us were five or six women clad in immense sacks which they called robes, and in which they seemed very much embarrassed. All around us was the population of Kaawaloa, lying flat upon the rocks, supporting the chin with their hands and gazing upon us with fixed attention. Kapiolani was entirely dressed in the European fashion; a gown of flowered English muslin, a sash of blue silk, and shoes, composed her toilet. Two tortoise shell combs secured her hair. On her fingers were three or four silver rings. The people around us formed as singular an assemblage as could anywhere be found. The only clothing of one was a watchcoat without buttons; of another, a shirt, and of a third, a pair of pantaloons; the most part were naked, with the exception of the indispensable *maro*. All the women, if not clothed, were at least covered. Some were clad like those mentioned above; the others, by far the greatest number, were merely enveloped in a sort of large shawl of Hawaiian cloth *(tapa)*.

Our conversation with Kapiolani was not long; the English sailor acted as interpreter. For the most part, a sort of grunt was the only reply she made to the long compliments which individuals of our party addressed her; yet there was upon her countenance a singular expression of kindness and natural goodness, and when we mentioned a desire to go to the upper village, on the morrow, to attend divine worship, the design appeared to give her great pleasure, and she offered to furnish us with horses and a guide.

On leaving Kapiolani we went to see the place where Captain Cook had been assassinated; it was where we landed. They pointed out to us the rock on which he was standing, when he received the fatal thrust. Looking around, we saw ourselves surrounded by the same people that had assassinated him.

The death of Cook was indeed a great misfortune; but perhaps it ought to be attributed only to himself and to the violence of his character; at least it so appeared this day. There has not been, nor is there now anything sanguinary in the character of this people, but they manifested an almost boundless respect for those foreigners, whom they considered as gods. There was need of all the horror, which the sacrilege committed by Cook, he seizing the king of the island, inspired, to urge them to this excess. We could see traces of the vengeance inflicted by the companions of Cook, after his death; they showed us cocoa-nut trees pierced by balls, and rocks shivered by the artillery.

The next day, we found at Kaawaloa the horses and guide which Kapiolani had promised. Horses were imported into the Sandwich Islands from California, and they began to be numerous. Some of the horses sent for our use were furnished with English saddles, and the others with clumsy Mexican saddles. The distance between Lower Kaawaloa and Upper Kaawaloa is about three miles. There is a very good road between the two places, leading up the side of the mountain. This road is due to the missionaries, who resorted to a singular expedient to accomplish the object. They caused a law to be enacted, by which every person, man or woman, convicted of adultery, should pay a fine of fifteen dollars (seventy-five francs), or in case of non-payment, should labor on the roads four months. The plan of the missionaries has been so much encouraged by the people, that this road was completed in less than two years, and that another road from Kaawaloa to *Kailua* (large town), a distance of about twenty-five miles, is almost finished; and so, thanks to the amorous propensities of the Hawaiians, we accomplished, very easily, the three miles which we had to pass over.

As we ascended, the appearance of the land changed. All these islands have evidently been formed by successive eruptions of submarine volcanoes; and as a proof of their origin, lava is everywhere found. It is seen near the shore such as it was, at the moment when it became hard. The different strata, one above another, can be distinguished; since, in proportion to the elevation, the lava, owing to the alternate action of heat and moisture, is more and more decomposed. On the table land where the rains are abundant, the lava is found changed into fertile soil; and there grows in abundance the *kukui* (candle-nut tree), from the nut of which is extracted a very clear oil, which is very good to burn.   This oil has already become an article of exportation. The bread-fruit tree, the orange, the mulberry (imported from Manila), the banana, the sugar cane, the taro *(arum esculentum)*, its root growing in the water, and which constitutes the principal food of the islanders, are also abundant. Through the crevices of the rocks escaped some dwarf shrubs, a species of the caper bush, the *nai-hi,* the root of which, as we were informed, serves the natives for tea.   There was also the *tapa,* from which they make their clothes, and the flower of which, of a saffron yellow, rivals in brilliancy the magnificent blue, white and red convolvulus which bordered the road.*

About midway between the two villages is the monument erected, in 1825, by Lord Byron, commandant of the English frigate *Blonde,* in memory of Cook. It is at the place where had been interred all that could be found of his scattered members; it is a post fixed in the midst of lava rocks, which have been piled up so as

---

*Barrot seems to have been misinformed with respect to the name and uses of the caper bush, as well as the meaning of *tapa*.   The caper bush was called *maiapilo* or *puapilo* and was not used for tea. *Tapa* is Hawaiian bark cloth, not a plant.

to form a sort of tumulus. A copper plate, upon which is engraved the name of Cook is fastened to the top of the post. The epitaph, which accompanies it, has become illegible. The post is covered with the names of English sailors, who came to render homage to the memory of the celebrated navigator. But this is a niggardly monument, and one is astonished that the English government has not been able to acknowledge, in a more suitable manner, the immense services rendered to navigation by Captain Cook. In the vaults of Westminster Abbey repose ashes, which have not so good a claim upon the gratitude of the people, as that which lies forsaken under the lava of Hawaii.

CHAPTER TWO

The house of Mr. Forbes is in the midst of a garden, which seemed to have been somewhat neglected, and surrounded by a quick-set hedge of *ki;* the ki is a shrub with large leaves, and its root when cooked has the taste of calomel or burnt sugar. The natives formerly extracted a very strong liquor from it, but at present the missionaries have prohibited, under severe penalties, the distillation of this root.

Mr. Forbes received us very cordially, and introduced us to his family, consisting of his wife, a native like himself, of the United States, and two lovely children. Kapiolani joined us and very soon the bell called us to church.

The church of Kaawaloa is in every respect like the houses of the country; it is a great shed in the form of a lofty cone, or rather, of a roof resting on the ground, the sides being supported by a frame held together by cords—for nails are not used in the construction of houses. This forms a sort of lattice work covered on the outside with the leaves of the *pandanus,* the cocoa-nut tree, or sugar cane. In the houses of the chiefs, the thatching is concealed by mats which line all the interior. The length of the church is about eighty feet, its width about forty, and its greatest height about fifty. It is capable of containing more than a thousand. About six hundred islanders were kneeling or sitting upon coarse mats. A number of chairs had been placed for us near the minister's pulpit. It was interesting to see this multitude assembled to hear the word of Christ, where, scarcely fifty years before, they offered human victims to abominable divinities. There are, it is true, very few real Christians among the natives, and almost all retain in the interior of their villages and of their houses, their absurd superstitions; yet it is much to induce them to come occasionally to hear words too mystical, without doubt, and of which they understand nothing, but which contain lessons of Christian morals so sublime, so simple and so well adapted to disclose to them, by degrees, the means of civilization. The men were on one side and the women on the other. No individual was admitted naked, but Mr. Forbes was obliged not to be too particular in respect to the form of the garment. For the most part, the men were enveloped in large pieces of native cloth in the manner of a cloak. Many of the women wore straw hats, and some were en-

veloped from head to foot in unbecoming cloaks such
as English females still wear in the country. Individuals
in the congregation had prayer books, printed at *Honolulu* and *Lahaina* in the Hawaiian language, and when
according to the Presbyterian form, Mr. Forbes commenced singing the psalms of the ritual, voices, hesitat-
ing at first, and then more confident, accompanied that
of the missionary. In fine, with the exception of some
want of attention, occasioned no doubt by our presence; with the exception of some enticing glances from
the women near us, all passed off decently—but it was
easy to perceive notwithstanding, that the great majority of the congregation were present by necessity.
Kapiolani was arrayed in her best; her dress was of black
satin, and she wore upon her head a cloak of native
fabric as glossy almost as satin. She seemed to follow
with attention the divine service in the book before
her; her countenance was not wanting in dignity, and
a pair of battered spectacles on her nose gave to her
an appearance which, even in Hawaii, appeared to us
very singular.

On the morrow, I went to visit the village of Kealakeakua, accompanied by M. Eydoux, surgeon of the corvette, and M. Hébert. To land with dry feet was impossible, and we were obliged to swim in some manner
in order to reach the shore. This failed not to excite
the mirthfulness of the population around us. It is
certain that the customs of the country were much
better adapted to the occasion than our own. A crowd
of boys and girls immediately surrounded us. Although

scarcely two miles distant from Kaawaloa, the population of Kealakeakua appeared to be far less under the influence of the missionary. We could perceive this without difficulty in the clothing of the islanders and in their conduct towards us. Here the *maro* was the only article of clothing worn by the men, and scarcely were the women better clad. But the manner in which the women received us proved beyond a doubt, that their actions were not so immediately under the control of Mr. and Mrs. Forbes as those of the inhabitants of Kaawaloa. They employed every possible art to attract our attention and to win our favor; but it is true that the rings and necklaces distributed by these gentlemen to the prettiest, were not without influence upon their friendly dispositions.

The itch seemed to be a prevailing malady among them, almost all were more or less affected with it. This circumstance, joined to the copper color of their skin and to the sluttishness of their clothing, diminished very much the strength of their attractions. As the men that we had seen up to that time seemed to have a preference for money and clothing, so the women at Kealakeakua appeared to have preserved the taste for toys noticed by the first navigators. A string of glass beads, a copper ring with a colored stone, filled them with joy.

Towards noon, the entire female population of Kealakeakua assembled to bathe in a small bay surrounded by lava rocks; one rock served the bathers for a screen, and they plunged thence entirely naked, into the waves which were breaking upon the shore; a plank, six or eight feet in length, and pointed at one end, enabled them to sustain themselves on the crest of the waves. It was indeed, a singular picture—a swarm of young women passing far out to sea, then returning with the swiftness of an arrow, borne upon the foaming crest of the surges which break with the noise of thunder on each side of the bay. I expected every moment to see them dashed against the sharp points of the rocks, but they avoided the danger with surprising address; indeed, danger seemed to delight them, and they dared to defy it with a courage which astonished me.† The least movement of their body gave to the plank which sustained them, the desired direction, and disappearing for a moment in the midst of the breakers, they very soon arose from the foam and returned at their ease to run the same race again. I saw a mother, who having placed her child, scarcely a year old, upon a plank two feet long, pushed it before her to a great distance, and then abandoning it to the fury of the waves, she followed, directing only now and then the plank which sustained it.

I had expected to see this population such as Capt. Cook found it, free and independent, and the contrast I avow, did not appear to me in favor of the present, when I afterwards saw these women covered with dirty rags.

The difficulties we had experienced in landing suggested the idea of returning on board the *Bonite* in a canoe. We had been able to appreciate during the day,

the advantages possessed by these light and easily
worked canoes in a rough sea over our heavy boats.
We entered a canoe of about fifteen feet in length and
a foot or more in width. This canoe, like all those of
the Pacific islands, had an out-rigger made of a piece of
light wood and fixed parallel to the canoe by means of
two transverse bars four or five feet in length. Our Indians waited for what is called a *calm,* that is the moment when the waves which usually succeed one
another to the number of four or five, seem to cease
for an instant, then they drew the canoe rapidly some
distance from the shore, when springing upon their seats
and paddling vigorously they were able before the next
wave rolled in to gain such a distance that we experienced only two or three strong undulations. We reached
the *Bonite* safe and sound.

The next day I spoke to Mr. Forbes concerning
the extraordinary dexterity in swimming which I had
observed on the preceding day among the natives.
"You can have no adequate idea of it," he replied,
"they are more at their ease in the water than on the
land." To confirm this assertion, he related an adventure which seemed too interesting to be omitted here.

The natives in their canoes frequently pass over the
channels which separate the different islands of the
archipelago. One day, a native accompanied by his wife
and two small children, put off in a canoe from the
northern point of Lanai with the design of landing on
the southern part of Molokai, a distance of seven or
eight leagues. When he had put to sea the weather was

fine, but suddenly a dark cloud blackened the sky, a gale commenced and the sea became very rough. For a long time the skill with which the islander guided his frail skiff in the midst of the waves preserved it from being wrecked; but at length a sea broke the out-rigger and the canoe capsized. The children were too young to be able to swim. He seized them at the moment when the sea was about to swallow them up, and placed them upon the canoe, which being made of light wood floated, although bottom up. Then he and his wife swimming at its side, undertook to urge it along to the nearest shore. They were then near the middle of the channel. After many hours of fatiguing exertion, and when they had almost reached the shore, they met a very strong current which urged them back into the open sea. To struggle against the force of the current would have been to expose themselves to certain death; they therefore decided to direct their canoe towards another part of the island. Yet the night came on and they began to feel cold. The woman was the first to complain of fatigue, but the desire so natural to escape death, and the sight of her children whose life depended upon the preservation of her own, gave her courage, and she continued to swim near her husband, pushing the canoe before them. Soon the poor children became fatigued for they could not long cling to the round and polished surface of the canoe without a continued effort, and they were also chilled with cold. Soon they relinquished their hold, and fell one after the other, into the sea. Their parents seized them and placed them again upon the canoe, striving at the same time to encourage them. Alas! their strength was exhausted—their little hands could no longer retain their grasp, and the sea engulfed them for the third time. It was no longer necessary to think of preserving the canoe; the parents therefore took the children upon their backs and swam towards the land which was scarcely visible in the darkness. An hour later, the woman discovered that the child which she was carrying was dead, and she broke forth into bitter lamentations. In vain did her husband persuade her to abandon the child and to take courage, pointing out to her the shore which now seemed near. The unhappy mother would not separate from her lifeless child, and she continued to carry her precious burden until she felt her strength nearly exhausted, when she told her husband that she must die, for she could swim no further; yet, notwithstanding her husband's earnest entreaties, she would not relinquish her burden. He then endeavored to sustain her with one hand and to swim with the other, but nature could not prolong the struggle, and she disappeared beneath the waves. The husband continued to swim on in sadness. The desire to save his surviving child alone sustained him. At length, after many hours of unspeakable hardship, and when almost dead, he reached the shore. His first care was to embrace the son he had saved, for he alone remained to him of his beloved family. But on taking him into his arms, he perceived that he was dead, and he fell senseless upon the sand. He was discovered at day-break lying prostrate on the shore by some fishermen. He revived, but he died soon after in consequence of his sufferings, and perhaps also from grief. He had been in the water eighteen hours.

We were at Kealakeakua six days, visiting the natives at their houses and collecting such information as seemed to possess any interest. We were informed that Kapiolani together with Kaahumanu, wife of Kamehameha, was the first to embrace the Christian religion, but her conversion was not very sincere at first. "For twelve years or more," said Mr. Forbes, "she was a very bad woman. She was constantly drunk and she had four or five husbands. Even after having received baptism, she retained two; and it was only in consequence of our expostulations that she came to the conclusion to have but one." At present she is a virtuous woman, and she has become the firmest defender of the moral and religious innovations on Hawaii. Kapiolani has given many proofs of great energy. It once happened that a sailor belonging to an American ship, was arrested and put in prison, having been convicted of the offence for which persons were sentenced to labor on the roads of Hawaii. The captain of the ship waited upon Kapiolani and threatened to fire the village unless the sailor should be instantly released. "Here is my law," said Kapiolani, "the sailor shall pay the fine of fifteen dollars or he shall work four months on the roads—the same as his associate in guilt. Now if you have the force, fire the village; but while Kapiolani lives, her law shall be executed in her country." The captain was obliged to pay the fine, in order to obtain the release of the sailor.

In spite of all the zeal of Mr. and Mrs. Forbes—and the latter participates in all the labors of her husband—the number of real Christians has scarcely increased in the district of Kealakeakua. Mr. Forbes being alone in this district, and his school at Kaawaloa demanding his uninterrupted attention, he has not the leisure to make distant excursions. Consequently his influence is scarcely felt at a short distance from Kaawaloa, and the natives retain almost all the superstitions of their old religion. I should have earnestly desired to visit those parts of the island where no missionaries reside, in order to see the natives in their nearest approaches to the primitive state; but my lot being found closely connected with that of the *Bonite*, even until my arrival at Manila, it was necessary to be content with seeing only those parts where civilization has penetrated.

Kapiolani treated me with great kindness; she made me a present of a magnificent *kahili*, a sort of feather broom. Among the chiefs this is a token of authority. She invited me to visit her house at the lower village, and also the one she was building at the upper village. The latter has the advantage of being near the missionary and it has assumed a certain European aspect. There was building on the same lot a stone house of two stories. Her house in the lower village, with the exception of the doors and windows, which have been enlarged, continues the same that it was before the discovery of the island. As a general thing, the houses of the natives are sufficiently comfortable; the floors are commonly covered with mats excellently braided, upon which they spread a bed of dry ferns. Formerly there was but a single room in a house, and that was used for a dining room, drawing room and bed chamber. The missionaries are now persuading the people to make divisions in their houses, and for this purpose they generally employ large curtains of *tapa* or of English calico. These separations form the sleeping apartments. The bed is composed of a great number of mats laid one upon another, so as to form an estrade, the coarsest being placed at the bottom. This place is *tabu* (prohibited) to all the world.

Near Kapiolani's house is the tomb of her husband —a large stone edifice with a roof of boards. This man was a powerful and very rich chief; but at his death, a son that he had by his first wife, took from Kapiolani almost all that she held from him, and she is now comparatively poor.

A few calabashes for *poi* (fermented paste made of taro), one or two *kahilis*, sometimes a line and some paddles, constitute the entire furniture of a Hawaiian house. Fish slightly salted and very often raw, and poi, comprise their principal food. I took a notion to taste of poi, but it seemed detestable. It possesses the color and consistence of starch and an acid taste is very perceptible. At Kealakeakua butcher's meat is never eaten. All that Europeans can find here to sustain animal life are fowls, pigs, cocoa-nuts and a few kinds of fruits.

The importation of intoxicating liquors is prohibited; we could however perceive that the islanders are not destitute of the fondness for ardent spirits, which has been observed, exists among all nations. Even the women opened their mouths with avidity to receive the brandy which we gave them. The islanders as a general thing, are restrained from giving themselves up to their old practices not by conviction of truth, but from fear of punishment. Whenever occasion offers they hasten to throw off the yoke which has been imposed upon them. Four or five months before, Kauikeaouli, King of the Sandwich Islands, with a part of his court, made a visit to Hawaii, and he gave himself up to excesses in which not only those who accompanied him took part, but the whole population of Kealakeakua also. Neither Kapiolani nor Mr. Forbes ventured to make the least remonstrance—they waited impatiently in their houses until the country should be delivered from the presence of the wicked.

CHAPTER THREE

During our stay at Kealakeakua we were visited by Kuakini, Governor of Hawaii and one of the principal chiefs of the Sandwich Islands. He resides at Kailua, and is well known by the name of "John Adams." He came in his double canoe, managed by a score of stout Indians. He is a man of six feet and three inches; a blue vest, grey pantaloons, shoes without stockings, and a straw hat, constituted his accoutrement. We had been previously informed concerning his fine uniform and his large epaulettes.

Kuakini speaks very good English, and has the reputation of being an intelligent but at the same time, an avaricious man. There was no proof, however, of his avarice in his sale of provisions to the *Bonite*. We were informed, it is true, that these provisions cost him nothing, except the trouble of sending his people for them

among the poor islanders; such is the custom of the
country the chiefs may lay claim to everything. Kuakini received from the corvette a certain quantity of
iron in bars and some tools. He was accompanied by
another chief named Hekili (*thunder*), not surpassed
by the Governor himself in stature. They came every
day on board the *Bonite*, the table and the wine of
which, having, no doubt, strong attractions for them.
Their appetite was insatiable, and in perfect keeping
with their immense corpulency. The wine of Bordeaux,
and more especially Muscat wine, seemed perfectly to
their taste, notwithstanding the temperance laws established in the country. We also had a specimen of the
influence exerted over this people by the missionaries.
Dining with us one day, in company with Mr. Forbes
and Kapiolani, Kuakini scarcely dared to pour the least
quantity of wine into his water; but when Mr. Forbes
was not present, he carefully avoided having any water
put into his wine. Yet Kuakini, they say, is utterly
opposed to the missionaries. He reads and understands
English very well, and accuses them of not having
translated the Bible faithfully. As to poor Kapiolani,
she never made the slightest gesture, without a glance at
Mr. and Mrs. Forbes.

The population of Hawaii scarcely amounts to
29,000. When discovered, it exceeded 90,000. The
causes of this fearful diminution we will investigate
before closing this article. The weather at the shore is
very warm, Fahrenheit's thermometer ranging generally
between eighty-six and eighty-nine degrees (about

twenty-five degrees of Reaumur's) while at the upper village the air was fresh and pure, a sea breeze was felt, and the atmosphere seemed entirely different.

On my first going ashore, I had observed numerous holes in the precipice which overlooks the bay. These holes seemed to me to be the work of the natives, nor was I deceived. They are sepulchres for their dead. The excavation is usually closed up with wood work. There is at the present time in the village where Mr. Forbes resides, a cemetery where those are buried who die in the Presbyterian religion.

The principal object of our coming to Kealakeakua was not accomplished; we were obliged to relinquish our design of exploring the summit of Mauna Loa. From all the information we could obtain, it was evident that in our circumstances, our intended expedition was impracticable. We were assured that it would take eight days at least, to reach the summit of Mauna Loa, and nearly as long a time to return. They represented, with exaggeration I doubt not, the dangers and obstacles we should meet with in our excursion. This last consideration could not have the least influence on the determination of the gentlemen who had planned the ramble; but time was wanting. The days of our stay at Hawaii were numbered; in two months we were under the necessity of being at Manila. We had to visit Oahu, the residence of the King. The ordinary chances of the sea might render our voyage much longer than we anticipated, and we were compelled to abandon our project. Our young officers, and especially M. Gaudichaud, the botanist of the expedition, regretted it exceedingly. Indeed, I was certain that the exploration of Mauna Loa would be followed with beneficial results, and that natural history would be enriched through the assiduity of Messrs. Eydoux and Gaudichaud, by a great number of interesting discoveries. As the snows on the summit of Mauna Loa and its famous crater, said to be twenty-five miles in circumference, had been for a long time the subject of our conversation and the object of our desires, we all lamented the necessity of the sacrifice.

Nothing can be more picturesque than Hawaii, as it appears from the sea. Near the shore it is very much broken and the soil appears everywhere covered with richest vegetation; but the eastern and northern part of the island is much more pleasant and fertile than the part we visited, which is almost entirely destitute of running water. The inhabitants of Kealakeakua are under the necessity of going five or six miles for their water, or else of drinking that which is brackish in no slight degree. Water might easily be conducted from the mountain to the sea by means of pipes; the rapid descent of land being very favorable, but a long time will pass before the inhabitants of this island can be in a condition to perform such a work. The eastern and northern parts of the island are well watered; there are many streams and many ponds of sweet water which serve as reservoirs for the regular inundations of the taro patches. The inhabitants of this part of the island are much more numerous than where we visited, and the climate is also better. It is in the eastern part that the famous volcano, Mauna Kea, raises its sublime head and by its frequent eruptions, keeps the inhabitants in a constant state of alarm. Here the Goddess *Pele* has her residence. The traditions concerning this divinity of the Sandwich Islands have been related in so interesting a manner by M. Dumont d'Urville in his *Voyage Around the World,* that I should only impair the poetic picture of this navigator by undertaking to repeat them.

We sailed Oct. 6th, and at noon we were off Kailua, the residence of Governor Kuakini, who had come on before us. The corvette lay to, and we went on shore. As we could remain only three or four hours, we wished to make the most of our time. We first went to visit the church, which was unfinished. It is built of stone, and is the work of an Englishman. It is one hundred and twenty-five feet in length, forty-eight feet in width, its walls are about twenty-four feet high and the height of the steeple is one hundred and thirty feet. The interior is finished with a good degree of elegance. It is furnished with a broad gallery of carved wood, containing seats for a part of the congregation. The pulpit or desk of the missionary is of *koa,* a wood slightly resembling mahogany. In fine, a person here might imagine himself in a European temple, and the most of our villages are far from having churches comparable to that of Kailua. Kuakini went with us to show us the church, appearing very proud of what he called his "monument," and evidently enjoying our admiration. He then took us to his house, which appeared very

much like that of Kapiolani. Extended curtains of
English calico concealed the secret apartments of the
women from vulgar eyes. Upon the estrade of honor,
was lying at full length, a gigantic woman, clad in a
gown of azure satin. I never saw any thing more monstrous or more hideous than this woman. It was Mrs.
Kuakini. Her height could not be less than five feet
and ten inches, and she was completely round. All
the chiefs that I have seen appear to belong to a gigantic race. To be small and lank is, with them, a mark of
low birth. M. Eydoux and myself passed among the
islanders for great personages, and we were much more
respected by them than if we had been destitute of such
a degree of corpulence as never fails to incommode us
in this hot latitude. To attain to this so much desired
corpulence, nothing can be better adapted than the
manner of living in vogue with the chiefs. They pass
their lives, so to speak, reclining on their mats; very
seldom do they take a walk, and they eat from morning
till night.

A numerous company surrounded the estrade of
honor. The young daughter of Kuakini was squatting
near her mother. A number of women were waving
kahilis above the princesses, in order to keep away the
flies, which, in revenge, came to devour us. The principal inhabitants of Kailua were reclining upon mats
around the room. Kuakini seated himself upon a
settee, and motioned us to take some chairs placed
near him. We were very thirsty, for the heat was excessive, and we had been two hours at least, in the

boat; but Kuakini did not seem to think of our wants. He who had received a thousand attentions every time he came on board, and who seemed to regard as excellent the wines which were always offered him, thought not to provide the refreshments we so much needed. We were under the necessity of asking him for water, and this decided him to order us some Madeira.

Before leaving we enjoyed the pleasure of seeing the Governor and his family take their dinner; but he was very careful not to give us an invitation. He perceived without doubt that we should find difficulty in adapting ourselves to his manner of eating, and truly, there is nothing more disgusting. A glance only at their food might suffice to drive appetite away. It consisted of baked pork, salted fish uncooked, and poi, which, among the islanders, is the staff of life—without poi, they do not make a single meal. Each sort of food was contained in an enormous calabash. Kuakini stretched himself at full length near his agreeable wife, and then commenced a sort of contest to see who should eat the most ravenously and with the furthest remove from neatness. Each, in turn, thrust his fingers into the calabashes for food. This surprised me, for at our table Kuakini had shown that he was far from being unacquainted with the use of knives, forks and spoons. One cannot imagine the quantity of pork, of fish and of poi, which this monstrous couple devoured. Were I to attempt to give an idea of it, I should be afraid of being charged with exaggeration. All the calabashes were emptied in a trice. The manner of eating poi, is this—plunging two fingers into the paste, they give the hand a circular motion until a sufficient quantity is collected, when it is conveyed to the mouth. During the repast, their attendants observed them with respectful silence. When the calabashes were emptied, a servant took the one which contained the poi—then collecting with his fingers the morsels that had been left adhering to the sides, he formed therewith a ball so attractive that Kuakini swallowed it in a twinkling.

We were so much the more surprised at Mrs. Kuakini's appetite, as her husband had just informed us that she was dangerously sick, and had requested Dr. Eydoux to see her. Her illness appearing to be simply the result of excessive corpulence and unbroken indolence, the Doctor recommended exercise and attention to diet, two prescriptions which it would be difficult for her to put in practice, as Kuakini informed us. That she could not move without difficulty, was sufficiently evident, and from the manner in which she devoured her dinner, half an hour after the Doctor's prescription, we could judge that she would not, voluntarily, impose any restraint upon her appetite.

After their Excellencies had finished their dinner, we went to visit the Fort, in which are about twenty pieces of artillery of different calibres, mounted on wooden carriages. In the interior of the fort is the *morai,* or sacred house, where are deposited the remains of Kamehameha, the founder of the present dynasty. Wooden gods, with unseemly features, are stationed as sentinels at the corners and seem to forbid approach. These are the last external vestiges of the old religion.

The aspect of Kailua, although considered the capital of Hawaii, did not give us a very favorable idea of the civilization of the inhabitants. A few huts, scattered here and there, without order or symmetry; a crowd of ragged men and women following us everywhere and watching even our slightest motions with fatiguing curiosity—this is what we found at Kailua, and what we were destined to find again at Honolulu, the capital of the Sandwich Islands, for which place we were about to sail.

At daybreak, Oct. 8th, we were in sight of Oahu, and at six o'clock we cast anchor outside of the reef, which forms the harbor of Honolulu. The appearance of Oahu is more pleasant than that of Hawaii; the land is more broken, less striking perhaps, but more varied, more verdant, and more picturesque. The town of Honolulu is situated on the seashore, in the midst of a rich plain, five or six miles long and two broad. We could perceive back of the town and upon the slopes of the hills, numerous taro patches. The town has a sort of European aspect. To the right of the harbor is a white-washed fort, through the embrasures of which we saw thirty cannons of all sizes, whose muzzles, painted red, seemed anything but formidable. In the midst of the scattered houses are seen a number of lookouts, steeples and cocoa-nut trees. We perceived at a distance, white fronts, green balconies and roofs built in the European manner, while the green hills which overlooked the harbor extended to the horizon. On our right were two craters, one of which is called the *Punch Bowl*; the summit of this is indented and forms embrasures, where cannon of a very large calibre have been stationed. On the right and left of the harbor are coral reefs, over which the sea breaks with violence and which are almost entirely covered at high water. Through these reefs is an opening seventy or eighty fathoms wide, and this is the entrance of the harbor. Natives were advancing on these reefs even to the breakers, where some were bathing, some fishing, and others were taking shell-fish.

Our arrival, as we were afterwards informed, occasioned the Government some alarm. It was supposed that we had come to demand satisfaction for the arbitrary sending away of the French Catholic Missionaries. Scarcely had we cast anchor, when the King's Secretary, accompanied by the American Consul and the Editor of the Oahu *Gazette* , came on board, in order, doubtless, to find out the real object of our arrival; for as soon as he was informed that our mission was of a peaceful character entirely, his countenance, which betokened much solicitude when he came on board, assumed a joyous expression.

Few canoes had put off from the shore to visit us, and it was easy to perceive that the arrival of a large ship, and even of a ship of war, was no new thing at Honolulu. We could already perceive a great difference in the clothing and manners of the natives. The

Secretary of the King wore a frock coat and a military cap; his watch-guard was a black ribbon, and his shirt of figured cambrick was becoming.

Honolulu has become the seat of Government; it is the entrepot of the commerce of the whole country. Of this we were convinced when, on our arrival, we saw at anchor many English and American ships discharging their cargoes, or taking on board the products of the islands. Yet it was the season when the smallest number of vessels are found in port; and we have since learned that the whalers, who come here for refreshments or repairs, generally arrive in November and February, and that sometimes there are thirty or forty ships in the harbor. The American sloop of war *Peacock,* bearing the broad pennant of Com. Kennedy, was in port; as also many Hawaiian vessels, among which we noticed a brig of American construction. This was the King's yacht, and was called *Harrietta*, after his sister—much better known by her true name, *Nahienaena*.

The Village of Kealakeakua

Lauvergne

CHAPTER FOUR

A wharf, built of large timbers and filled in with stone, rendered our landing easy, and we found ourselves in the capital of the Sandwich Islands. We were immediately surrounded by this idle population, for the employment of which civilization has as yet found no means. They were, as on Hawaii, covered with rags and the itch; but it was a sight to which we had become accustomed, and it no longer surprised us. The population of Honolulu had an appearance of neatness more general than the people of Hawaii, but there was something in them more repulsive. The men appeared more polite, but at the same time, more deceitful, and vice seemed to have set a mark upon the faces of the women. I enter into these details because I am speaking of a people which has had intercourse with European nations scarcely sixty years. There ought to be some interest in seeing the moral and physical changes which this people has experienced, and here opens to our observation a vast and fertile field.

The town of Honolulu does not appear attractive on close inspection. The houses around the landing place are merely cabins, built in the ancient style of the country. From them came out a crowd of ragged women and children to see us pass. Leaving the fort on our right, the white walls of which were set off by the thatched roofs around, we made our way into the town. The streets were sufficiently wide and quite straight. We saw a number of pretty European dwellings, some public places, and a number of well cultivated gardens.

The contrasts before our eyes could not but greatly interest us. This constant mingling of civilization and barbarism, produced a singular effect. Here passed a chaise in which were a gentleman and lady, the complexion of the latter giving evidence that she was born in the Sandwich Islands. Further on, a native, whose only covering was a *tapa* mantle fastened by a knot on his right shoulder, was mounted, without saddle, upon a mettlesome horse which he managed skillfully. In a court, a number of white children dressed in the European manner, ornamented frocks and calico pantaloons, were engaged at their sports; and near them was shining in the sun, the naked and brown skin of native children, whose only garment was the indispensable maro. Here spacious stone houses presented to view the products of European industry; and at the gate, an Indian, clothed, and with a garland of banana leaves around his head, stopped us in order to dispose of some land shells, lobsters or birds. Sometimes we could distinguish, through the half opened blinds, the elegant scarfs and fair countenances of ladies who were watching the newly arrived as they passed in the midst of a throng of islanders, who, with dishevelled hair and naked limbs, endeavored by fixing upon us their roguish eyes, to provoke some mark of attention.

There are three churches in Honolulu. The most important of these is the Seamen's Chapel, where the aristocracy of the country, the white population, worship on the Sabbath. Under the same roof is a reading room, where are found, often of remote date it is true, the principal newspapers of the civilized world. Adjoining the reading room is the cabinet of natural history, all the specimens of which are confined to some shells of the country and the coast of California, and to a dozen bows and arrows from the Fiji Islands. The second church is that of the natives, and this, without dispute, has the most interest for a European. It was in this church that I attended divine service; but as I have already spoken of a similar service on Hawaii, I will only say that here the costumes were not so singular as at Kaawaloa. The church itself, built of stone, with its steeple, and its bell, its carved pews and its seats already polished by age, could not be compared with the church of Kaawaloa, with its walls and roof of thatch, its timbers bare and held together by cords, its mats and its modest desk. The native population were in their best attire, and in the crowd we noticed numerous hats very comically worn, and hoods shading coarse and brown faces which needed not this ornament in order to be singular. There were scenes there truly worthy of the pencil of Hogarth.

The next day after our arrival, we made a visit in due form to the King. He received us in the house of his sister, Nahienaena. It was because his own house was at some distance that he received us here, and he did not wish to compel us to take a long walk under a burning sun. This house, like all those of the country, contained but a single room, the partitions having been removed. A large estrade of fine mats occupied the further end of the.hall. The walls on the inside as well as the ceiling or roof, were covered with mats, to which were appended green branches for the purpose of attracting the flies and relieving the company from their annoyance. In front of the estrade, sitting in arm-chairs, were the King, Kauikeaouli, and the three sisters and wives of Rihoriho, his brother and predecessor. A number of chairs to complete the circle, had been placed for us. Behind the King and Princesses were the principal chiefs, some of them standing and some reclining upon the estrade. The chiefs were in uniform. We were presented by the Governor of the fort. His Hawaiian Majesty wore a blue coat with military buttons, and large epaulettes. He is about three or four and twenty years of age; his countenance is expressive, although somewhat marred by a broad flat nose and thick lips.

He is strongly made, and is about five feet, three or four inches in height. He received us very cordially; but we imagined that we perceived in him a certain embarrassment, which probably resulted from the apprehension occasioned by our arrival, or perhaps from his being little accustomed to formal presentations. This embarrassment, however, gradually disappeared, and his countenance assumed an expression of frankness and good humor. Kinau, widow of Rihoriho, and regent during the minority of Kauikeaouli, was seated at his right; at his left was Kekauluohi, another widow of Rihoriho, and at the right of Kinau, a third widow of Rihoriho, called Liliha.

Of the many sons of Kamehameha, the first king of the Sandwich Islands, Rihoriho and Kauikeaouli are the only ones concerning whom we have any information. After the death of Kamehameha, Rihoriho was called to the throne under the regency of Kaahumanu, his mother. Rihoriho died in England. Why he went to that country is not well known. He had five wives, three of whom were his own sisters, and the other two half sisters. His favorite wife died in England a little before himself. A second wife died at Maui not long after. Three widows of Rihoriho survive, and these were the three women before us. Kauikeaouli succeeded Rihoriho, and at Kaahumanu's death, which occurred during the minority of Kauikeaouli, the regency devolved upon Kinau, who occupied the highest rank among the surviving widows of Rihoriho. She retained the power till Kauikeaouli became of age; but it would appear that her influence outlived her office, and that, being herself completely under the authority of the American Missionaries, she exercises an absolute control over the young king.

The princesses were arrayed in silk, and by their size, reminded me of Mrs. Kuakini. To see three women of such immense corpulence seated together in a saloon, would certainly be considered a monstrous thing in Europe. The smallest was at least five feet seven or eight inches in height, and they seemed to vie with each other in presenting the largest circumference to the admiration of the vulgar. Corpulence, as I have already remarked, is a mark of distinction on the Sandwich Islands, and few women surely could lay claim to greater eminence in this respect, than those before us. The King, although very athletic, cannot compare with his sisters in plumpness, and as he is accustomed to ride on horseback, to fence, and take other exercise, it is doubtful if he ever becomes a *great* man, according to the Hawaiian acceptance of the term.

We were received very politely by the whole court. The King speaks English very well; but as the commander of the *Bonite* was not familiar with this language, and still less with the Hawaiian, the conversation, of necessity, languished. During all this interview, the King, as I imagined, before replying to a question, consulted Kinau. The expression of her countenance and the vivacity of her glance, betokened an absolute character.

Mr. Charlton, the English consul, who had accom-

panied us, inquired of the King if it would be agreeable
to him to have his portrait taken by some officers of
the corvette who were present.   He assented, after
having exchanged glances with Kinau. The young gentlemen set about the work, and in half an hour, they
had sketched with a good degree of accuracy, the portraits of the King and Princesses. On their examining
the portraits, each of the women appeared only half
satisfied with her own portrait; but each laughed hearti-
ly on viewing those of her sisters. The interview ended
by a promise from the King to visit the *Bonite* on the
morrow.

On the 11th, he came on board, accompanied by
Kinau and many officers. He was in full Windsor costume, with white plumes in his hat. This suit of clothes
was a present from George IV. It was not without
fear, as we were informed, that he came on board the
French corvette. He also apprehended at one time
while on board, that some violence would be inflicted
on him in order to obtain reparation for the act which I
have already mentioned. This information was probably false; at any rate, the distinguished reception which
he received on board the *Bonite*, must needs have
allayed his fears, if indeed he had experienced any. He
wished to see everything in detail and requested to wit-
ness the cannon and musket exercise—but what amused
him most, was the staff exercise, in which many of our
sailors were adept.

Kauikeaouli's tastes, from what we could observe,
are altogether martial. He is somewhat acquainted with

naval matters, and pointed out the difference between
the rigging of the corvette and that of other ships, which
he had seen. He often makes excursions to the neigh-
boring islands in his brig, the *Harrietta,* and he managed her, in part, himself. Unfortunately, his education
is very defective, and the missionary Bingham, whose
pupil he is, seems to have made it his business to shut
up his mind from those branches of knowledge which
would have been the most necessary for him to learn in
order to govern well. He is also, as I have already said,
completely under the influence of his sister-in-law,
Kinau, who rules in his name. He possesses, nevertheless, intelligence and memory, and his questions, sometimes judicious, indicate an ardent desire of knowledge.
The time will perhaps come, when he will seize the
reins of empire and call Kinau to account for her
administration, and the missionaries for their counsels.
The King and his suite left the *Bonite* perfectly satisfied with their reception, and with what they had
seen.

Some days after, the King proposed to make a
feast for the officers of the *Bonite*, and he requested
Mr. Charlton to give me an invitation. Upon this I
congratulated myself, for the feast was to be in the
country, two leagues from Honolulu, and was to be, as
they told us, disencumbered of all etiquette. We were
to have a dinner in a grove, and then songs and ancient
dances of the country—the singers and dancers were to
be clothed in the ancient costume. I looked forward
to the appointed day with impatience. It came at last.

We met at the King's house. We set out at ten o'clock, forming a cavalcade of thirty or forty persons. In front was the King, mounted upon a beautiful white horse, and surely it would have been difficult at the time, to find a better or more elegant horseman. We rode on, without order, and if the native horsemen excited our curiosity, we afforded them amusement also by our manner of riding. Some of our young officers took their first lesson in horsemanship on this day, and at the end of half an hour or more, their movements were no more easy than at the moment of their starting. On the contrary, all the natives who accompanied us were excellent equestrians. The servants of the King, mounted on horses without saddles, brought up the rear. They reminded me, by their steadiness and even by their graceful attitudes, of those Roman knights we have seen upon ancient engravings.

Thus we proceeded six or seven miles in the midst of a green valley, shut in between two mountains, which seem to have been once joined together so much analogy and resemblance was there between the opposite irregularities. On our right was a river, or rather a torrent. Concealed for the most part from our eyes, we occasionally saw its silver cascades leaping from the black lava rocks. We could judge of the fertility of the valley, from the rich plantations of taro on all sides of us. This root, less farinaceous than the potato, must be exceedingly productive; for a little spot not more than five rods square, as I was informed would sustain the year round, a family of seven or eight persons. On our right and left were scattered cabins, from the doors of which peered forth the brown faces of the owners. A dense herbage covered the uncultivated parts of the valley, and the mountains seemed to be covered with the kukuis, the silver foliage of which contrasted finely with the dark rocks from the midst of which it sprung.

At length we reached the end of our excursion. During our ride we had been constantly ascending, almost insensibly at first, and then towards the extremity of the valley we found ourselves in the midst of precipices which the King ascended and descended with remarkable intrepedity. And now if the only object of our excursion had been the magnificent spectacle before us, we should have been more than paid for our trouble. Rising to a very great height above us, were the threatening summits of the mountains, whose dry and naked peaks seemed ready to fall on our heads. Behind us, stretched the valley of Honolulu, and beyond, the sea and the ships in the harbor. At our feet, and at a depth of two or three thousand feet perpendicular, we saw the tops of the trees which border the beautiful valley of Kaneohe.

This valley extends with a gentle inclination to the sea, which, on that side of the island, as well as the other, furnishes for the picture a frame of breakers. It would be impossible to sketch with the pencil, and much more so, to describe with words, the varieties of scenery so great and so picturesque, which makes from this point of view one of the most magnificent panoramas that nature can offer to the enthusiasm of her admirers. We were upon the wall of mountains, which divides the island into two equal parts. We were at the *Pali*. This is a place celebrated in the history of the Sandwich Islands. It was here that His Majesty's father, Kamehameha, who subdued all the chiefs of the adjacent islands and who attained to absolute power, gained his last victory. This is the Thermopylae of Oahu. Here the king of Oahu, vanquished and a fugitive, preferred a voluntary death to the cruel fate which the conqueror had designed for him. He precipitated himself, they say, from this perpendicular wall, together with all his warriors who had escaped the weapons of the enemy. It is said that Kamehameha stationed a guard behind his troops, that all hope of escaping death by flight being taken away, his soldiers might fight with greater courage.

From the top of the Pali we saw the preparations for our dinner. The inhabitants of the valley were scrambling up the foot path that winds along the side of the mountain, bearing on their heads the provisions which the King's attendants had demanded of each one; for, at the Sandwich Islands, the king is absolute master of the fortunes of his subjects. A roof covered with leaves had been raised during the night. Green ferns were spread on the ground, then a cloth, and upon this cloth were arranged European bottles, plates, etc. All this show of civilization did not please me, I acknowledge; it was too much like a dinner of our good citizens of Paris upon the greensward of Montmorency. I should have preferred the old Hawaiian manner. But it

was necessary to be satisfied with what we had.   I
noticed that the porcelain was of English manufacture,
and the table cloth was American.   These two nations
have in reality invaded the whole commerce of America
and India.   Dinner was announced, and we all reclined
upon the ferns.   At the King's order the *luau* was
served up.   A gastronomic feast is called *luau* in the
Sandwich Islands.   It takes its name from an indispensable dish of young taro leaves boiled or cooked in fat.
In an instant, the cloth was covered with young pigs,
fowls, fish, sweet potatoes, luau, etc.—all these having
been enveloped in leaves and cooked in the earth by
means of red hot stones.   We were all pleased with the
excellent relish of what was spread before us.   The fish
especially, cooked in taro leaves, was delicious, and we
were all constrained to acknowledge that we had never
eaten anything so good.   One thing only seemed wanting.   We had anticipated being regaled with the flesh of
the dog, but we were disappointed.   The missionaries
probably have forbidden the use of this viand.   One of
my neighbors, however, whispered in my ear his sus-
picions that one of the pigs lying before us without a
head belonged to a nobler genus.   It is said that the
flesh of these dogs, which are exclusively fed on fish and
poi, is exactly like that of pigs.   Besides, the natives
do not eat every species of the dog, one only having
been set apart for this purpose, and this was the terrier
species, with a long nose, short hair and short ears.
       The serving was performed with a good degree of
skill.   A crowd of waiters surrounded us; some clad in

pantaloons and vests, and others wearing the cool and commodious livery of the country. I noticed that always before serving up a dish, they opened the leaves which enveloped it, and took a morsel with their fingers, to taste it. I was informed that this was the practice at the King's table, and that nothing was served up there without having been tasted by the servants.

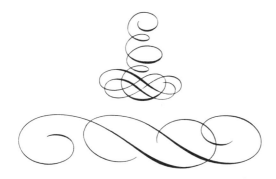

A Dance Scene in the Sandwich Islands

Lauvergne

CHAPTER FIVE

Madeira and Bordeaux wines circulated freely, and healths were drunk in the English manner, and gaiety reigned during the repast. We proposed the health of Kamehameha III, and he returned the compliment by proposing the health of *His Majesty, Louis Philippe, King of the French*. Our luau was then, the place excepted, very much like a European dinner. About thirty of us were at the table; no ladies were present. Among the guests I noticed the two sons of a Frenchman, who has been established many years at the Sandwich Islands as a sail-maker. The two young gentlemen spoke English fluently, and one of them had the kindness, after dinner, to interpret for me the songs of the natives. Opposite to me was Leleiohoku, son of Kalanimoku. He is better known by the name of Pitt.

He was baptized in 1819 or 20 on board the French corvette *Uranie,* commanded by M. de Freycinet. Kalanimoku was generalissimo and first minister of Kamehameha. Considering the country and the period in which he lived, he was a wonderful man. Leleiohoku is now one of the principal chiefs; he has married Nahienaena, sister of the King.

After dinner, we all mounted our horses again and started for the King's country house, where we were to hear Hawaiian songs and to see Hawaiian dancing. On our way to the Pali we had left this house on the right. Everything had been previously arranged; mats were spread in front of the cottage, and chairs were placed in a circle, and first, five singers appeared and kneeled down. Each of them was armed with a large calabash, which was made thin towards the middle; this calabash, held in the left hand by a string, aided the expression of their gestures in a singular manner. They were naked to the waist; their arms and breast were tattooed, and loose folds of tapa of various colors covered the lower part of their bodies. Their songs were a sort of recitative, or of modulated conversation, animated or slow, as the subject required.

The theme they had chosen, or which had been suggested to them, was an eulogy of the King. They spoke at first of the love which his people had for him. "A flower," said they, "grows upon the mountain height. When the stars hide themselves, and the sun comes out from the sea, it turns of itself and holds out its cup for the morning dew. We climb to the mountain's summit and pluck the flower that we may bear this health-giving dew to Kauikeaouli."

Then they extolled his prowess in war. "His horse turns his head to look at him, for he knows that he does not bear a common man. His lance is always red with the heart's blood of his enemies, and his battle-axe bristles with the teeth of warriors, who have fallen under his blows. When he speaks, his voice is heard beyond the mountains, and all the warriors of Oahu hasten to range themselves around him, for they know, that under such a chief, their feet will speedily tread in blood."

It may be perceived that Hawaiian poets also indulge in some license, and that court flatterers are everywhere the same. Kauikeaouli listened to it all with the greatest indifference.

But what was admirable in this song, which however had a compress of only two or three notes, was the perfect accordance with which the five singers spoke and gesticulated. They must have rehearsed many times to attain to this degree of perfection. Each one of the five pronounced, at the same time, the same note, the same word, made the same gesture, and moved his calabash in the most perfect time, either to the right or to the left, or striking it against the ground he caused it to give forth sounds somewhat similar to those of a bass drum. It might be said that they were all moved by the same impulse of thought and will. Sometimes the gestures varied and became inconceivably rapid, yet I was never able to discover a mistake. The voice, the hands, the fingers, the calabashes, the bodies of the five singers were always extended, moved, regulated by a spontaneous movement.

These singers were succeeded by three others, who were clad like the former, but garlands of leaves encircled their foreheads, while strings of the yellow fruit of the *pandanus odorantissimus* ornamented their necks and arms. All three were of admirable proportions, and of a beauty of countenance seldom seen on these islands. They sang of love and pleasure, of love, Hawaiian in its characteristics, a little too material, perhaps, and which was expressed by gestures none too modest. Pleasure the most sensual was indicated by the looks, the gestures, the words, and even the tones of these young men. At one time their countenances became dark, they waved with violence the feather fans which they held in the left hand, and the base of which, formed of a small calabash filled with shells and struck by the right at regular intervals, performed the office of castanets. Thus they sung the frenzy of jealousy.

Their song, like that of the first singers, was nothing more than an animated conversation. No other song, in fact, is known at the Sandwich Islands.

The instrumental music of the islanders, which is still found at a distance from the ports, and some vestiges of which we observed on Hawaii, consists of tamtams and a sort of flute with two holes. Instead of the lips, the nose is used in blowing this instrument, a graceful way, forsooth. The notes given forth by this instrument are not more varied than those of their vocal music.

The dancing was, at length, announced. But the time is past when the swarms of male and female dancers assembled on the green grass, and there, in their graceful dances accompanied by songs, recounted the glorious achievements of warriors. Singers and dancers were the historiographers of the country. In their memory the ancient traditions were preserved. The details of a war formed the subject of a song, and from the songs of the ancient Hawaiian bards have navigators drawn materials for their descriptions. It is then with regret that I have seen these national songs prohibited, under the pretext of their being profane. As well almost, might Homer and Virgil be prohibited! Dancing has also fallen into great disfavor in consequence of missionary influence. The dance which we witnessed felt the effects of this disposition.

Only one female dancer appeared. Formerly, graceful and easy, the upper part of the body of these dancers was entirely naked. Pieces of cloth, suspended from the hips, and hanging in graceful folds, imparted a sort of originality to their movement. Necklaces composed of the fruit of the pandanus, garlands of leaves or of feathers, bracelets of teeth either of the dog or whale encircling the arms and legs, and shaking in regular time, composed their apparel. The one who presented herself before us, wore a calico shirt. Her dancing appeared monotonous. She sung at the same time, and a singer behind her lent the assistance of his song and marked the time, by striking a calabash against the ground. Only one thing appeared remarkable in this dance; and that is, that the dancer regulated the measure and from time to time gave to the musician the subject of his song. The musician endeavored to make his time accord with the movements of her feet, and he succeeded with remarkable precision. Yet, at the end of half an hour, the dance began to seem long. The King perceived that we were becoming weary, and, as it had not been possible to procure other female dancers, we listened to a few more songs, after which we mounted our horses to return to Honolulu.

We had spent the day agreeably; yet we had been disappointed. This King of the Sandwich Islands, clad in vest and pantaloons, these chiefs apparelled in the European manner, this serving almost European, these common and familiar manners had the power almost of making us believe that we have just passed some hours in the society of one of the lower classes of a civilized nation. Then, again, the dancing, so mean and monotonous, was far from realizing the ideas we had formed of it. Only the singing and singers appeared to have preserved all the originality of ancient times. The picturesqueness of the scene, however, did not diminish. Behind us, a cottage built in the aboriginal style of architecture; around us, a crowd of Indians, naked or clad in the most fantastic costumes; before us, the singers seated upon mats, with their characteristic countenances and their strange songs; the sea appearing in the horizon, and in the midst of us a grove of green trees enamelled with flowers. All this together formed a charming picture, which exercised the pencil of our artists in copying.

Formerly the women were passionately fond of these sports and these public dances. Many females even of the royal family had the reputation of being finished actresses; for this people once had plays, and the members only of distinguished families appeared on the stage. Now, this taste has yielded to the counsels of the missionaries. Perhaps also the fear of their reprobation alone prevents the women from giving themselves up to their old practices; at any rate, we were completely excluded from the society of the ladies of the King's family.

On the morrow the King gave us, in the city, a repetition of what we had seen the day before; but the fascination of the country and of novelty was lacking, and the soiree was dull enough. Still, justice requires us to say that the King did his best to render our stay at Honolulu agreeable. His urbanity was extreme, and his good humor never failed for an instant. Every time that we went to see him he gave us the most cordial welcome, and seemed delighted to receive us.

I called one day with Mr. Charlton, on Nahienaena, the King's sister. When informed that she was only twenty years of age, I was surprised; she seemed to me much older. She was, however, hardly recovered from a long and wasting sickness. She received us very graciously. Like all the distinguished women of the country, she is very large; and she must needs be very fat in her ordinary state of health. We admired the smallness and elegant form of her feet and hands. She was surrounded by women of honor, among whom we observed a daughter of the Englishman Young, who had been taken by Kamehameha from an English ship, on board of which he was boatswain. He attached himself to the fortunes of this conqueror, and died at Honolulu seven or eight years ago, at the age of 95 years. He was interred in the tomb of the kings, and his sons hold, at the present time, a very distinguished rank in the country.

Mr. Charlton accompanied me one day in a call upon the favorite mistress of Kauikeauouli. The history of the amorous chief King with this woman is quite romantic. He was obliged to remove her, so powerful had the influence of the missionaries already become in this country, where twenty years since the Christian name was hardly known. Yet, in spite of their severe reprimands, he lives with her in concubinage, her birth being too obscure to allow of his marrying her.

The evening preceding our departure, we witnessed at the residence of Mr. Charlton, an exhibition altogether foreign: this was an Indian dance. The performers were from the N. W. coast of America. One of the vessels engaged in the commerce carried on between these Islands and that coast was in port, and had a score of those Indians on board. The consignee had the kindness to have them arrayed in the costume of their country, and in the evening, by the light of kukui nut torches they gave us a representation of their warlike and re-

ligious dances. This was certainly the most savage
display that we saw at the Sandwich Islands. Grotesque
figures painted with vermillion, feathers inserted in the
lips and in the gristle of the nose, the costumes, the
yells, the postures, the gestures, all combined to give us
a vivid idea of a savage dance; but these poor fellows,
accustomed to an extraordinary degree of cold in the
latitude of 50 and 55 degrees, appeared to us to suffer
exceedingly from the heat, and we exerted ourselves in
their behalf.

Honolulu already numbers four or five hundred
foreign residents, while at Kealakeakua there is only one
or two. Almost all, who possess any claim to respect-
ability, are Americans, and the commerce of the Sandwich Islands is almost exclusively in the hands of
Americans. But the laborers and mechanics are generally Englishmen. We everywhere received the most cordial welcome, and all the world was eager to feast us.
Hardly a day passed during all the time of our stay at
Honolulu, without our having been invited by someone
to a dancing or musical soiree; but the passengers and
officers of the corvette were almost the only dancers
and musicians. Much more than this, surely, ought to
be expected in a city of the Sandwich Islands. Among
all those persons, the recollection of whom we shall retain, I will mention the family of Mr. Charlton, the
English consul, whose open hospitality rendered my
stay at Honolulu infinitely agreeable, and who furnished
me with much interesting information. Nor shall I
soon forget Don Francisco Marini, who arrived at these

islands 40 years ago. Having attached himself to the fortunes of Kamehameha, he accompanied him in the long wars which he was under the necessity of carrying on, in prosecuting his conquests. He told us of the many wounds he had received, and of the great valor he had displayed in the divers battles, in which he had been engaged. We were also informed concerning some singular adventures which had befallen him.

One day Kamehameha fell dangerously sick. A Frenchman, by the name of Rives, was his physician. I know not whether the great King had received some intimation similar to that which furnished to Alexander the occasion of such an admirable proof of the confidence he reposed in his physician, or whether he had no great faith in the skill of his Esculapius. Be this as it may, he ordered him to prepare double potions of his remedies, and then made Marini take one of the potions, and not until he had seen the effect produced by the medicine upon the poor patient, would he consent to swallow his part. But Marini was far from having any confidence in the medical skill of Dr. Rives, who, as he well knew, was anything but a physician. Of necessity, therefore, he had as ardent a longing for the recovery of Kamehameha as Kamehameha himself, and never, perhaps, did a courtier wish good health to his King so sincerely as poor Marini.

But he met with another adventure much more tragic. Kamehameha commanded him, one day, to cut off a prisoner's head, and Marini was obliged to obey, using for this purpose a carpenter's saw. Someone wished to know if this anecdote was true, and asked him about it; a shudder seemed to pervade the body of the Spaniard. "Alas!" said he, "what could I do? If I had not cut off the prisoner's head he would have cut off mine. It is better to eat the head of a wolf than to be eaten by him."

Yet Kamehameha was not naturally cruel. It was he who abolished the custom, handed down from time immemorial, of slaughtering the prisoners after the battle. He also abolished the horrid practice of putting those to death, who, through inadvertence or ignorance, had entered a *tabu* or sacred place.

Yet Marini had lived very happy at the Sandwich Islands. He has had 52 children; but he was not, I imagine, so much in favor of monogamy as Goldsmith's good vicar. I inquired of him if he had any hope or idea of returning to Europe. "God only knows," he replied. "I should like very much to see my country again; but without doubt all my relatives are dead, and I should no more find there a single friend. Moreover, since I have become accustomed to this country, I live here happy and tranquil. As I am 65 years old, it is too late to form new habits. When I arrived here, this country was very fine. That was a good time for Europeans. The manners were simple and unaffected, and foreigners were respected. That time has passed. Savage men have become civilized, and civilized men have become savages. The missionaries have spoiled everything," added he, lowering his voice and looking to the right and left to see if anyone was within hearing; "they have changed the character of the population. They have occasioned bigotry and hypocrisy, which was once unknown among us." Then, fearing perhaps lest he had said too much, he added, "But without doubt, their institutions are good. They believed that they were doing good."

I talked a long time with this honest man, for I was interested in his conversation. He has seen the origin of civilization at the Sandwich Islands, and he has witnessed its development, every day, even to its present state. He has lived here a long time, free and happy, without any other restraint than that imposed upon all men by natural law, and by the instinct of good and evil. Some disagreeable incidents have scarcely cast a shade upon his life. At the present time, he sees a religion, which is not his own, invading the country, ruling it, and subjecting it to its own demands. He himself cannot leave the narrow circle which this religion has drawn around the population. He sighs for the liberty of conscience and of worship which he has enjoyed for forty years. When he reflects upon the past, he thinks that he may justly complain of the present and dread the future. Nor is it astonishing that he is discontented. It is said, however, that he is rich, and that, in consequence of his strict economy, his fortune is daily increasing.

CHAPTER SIX

During my stay at Honolulu, I made a number of excursions in the vicinity. The valley, in the midst of which Honolulu is situated, is truly magnificent, and it could be made to produce our colonial supplies in abundance. The hills around might be cultivated, and they would produce excellent coffee and cotton of superior quality. One day I took a delightful ride with Mr. Grimes, an American merchant. About a mile from the town, we left the road which extends along the shore, and directed our course towards the hills. We ascended by a very tolerable path. On reaching the summit of a hill, Mr. Grimes stopped his horse to enjoy my admiration. And surely it is difficult to imagine a prospect more picturesque and more enchanting. Behind us, the sun was disappearing in the ocean. Before us, shut in between two high mountains, the fantastic shapes of which were figured in profile on the azure of the sky, stretched a cool and verdant valley divided by a stream, which was hastening on through plantations of taro and sugar cane. In the middle of the valley were about fifty cabins, shaded by kukui and bread fruit trees; beasts were grazing in the meadows; the shade of the mountains extending over the whole valley; and the air was fresh and fragrant. The hill from which we enjoyed this prospect, rose on our left by an almost imperceptible slope, and a fine and gilded herbage covered it like a velvet carpet; around us, everything was silent; nothing was heard except the chirping of some birds, as they flew over our heads. We remained there until night came to conceal from us this ravishing spectacle. Were my residence in Honolulu, I should often come to meditate in the valley of Manoa.

Although European luxury has begun to appear in Honolulu, yet very few carriages are to be seen. The king has a carriage which he never uses. A few of the European and American residents have chaises and coaches. The rich chiefs, and especially their wives, who on account of their corpulence seem unable to walk, are seen riding about in hand-carts drawn by men. I recollect having met in the streets of Honolulu, the Governor of Maui and his wife making their visits. They were lying flat, side by side, supporting their chins with both hands, and their immense bodies tossed about by the motion of the vehicle, reminded me of certain carts which come to us from Sceaux or from Poissy. A throng of servants preceded and followed them; one carrying a parasol, another a fly-brush, and a third, the heir of this noble family. The men who drew this interesting couple, moved on at a brisk trot, the team being composed of at least eight or ten robust fellows, who from time to time were relieved by others.

The Governor of Maui stopped to talk with me, and, thanks to Mr. Charlton with whom I happened to be at the time, he made me understand that there would be on the morrow a grand review of the troops and of the militia in front of the king's house, and he invited me to be present.

Unwilling to lose so fine an opportunity of seeing the military forces of his Hawaiian Majesty, I was punctual to the appointment. Three hundred men, composing the entire army of the line, were drawn up in three lines. Each man was armed with a musket of English or American manufacture, without a bayonet. I shall not undertake to describe their costumes, for I should never get through. I could have wished that one of our inspectors general of infantry had been present. Of some, the only article of clothing was the *maro* about the loins; others wore upon their shoulders large pieces of cloth falling ostentatiously in folds, in the Roman fashion; and others had the head and body partly covered with leaves of the cocoa and banana formed into festoons.

Opposite the army of the line, and drawn up, also in three ranks, was the militia of Honolulu. To distinguish the regular troops from these would have been difficult; for there was no difference in their clothing. Few of the militia had muskets, and from the manner of using these, it was easy to perceive that they had not derived much advantage from the lessons of exercise which they had received. In front of the palace gate were stationed the royal guards, consisting of eleven men, dressed uniformly in pantaloons and white calico vests with scarlet facings. Each man was armed with a musket and bayonet. This was without dispute the elite of the army of Oahu. They seemed to hold the soldiers of the line and the militia in the most profound contempt, while from their proudly erect attitude and from their military bearing, it could be easily perceived that they were wonderfully impressed with the idea of their superiority.

The beating of the drum announced that the exercise was about to commence. An officer read a long discourse, not one word of which could I understand. I was informed afterwards, that many men having been absent from the last parade, the adjutant was exercising his eloquence on this subject. The exercise at length began, and surely, without excepting even the royal guards, the Hawaiian soldiers appeared to me somewhat deficient in expertness. But this however, is a science which they will learn soon enough. There are many things much more useful than military exercise which they could and should have been taught a long time ago, and of which they have not yet acquired the least idea. The orders were given in English. The last orders were, "Kneel—ground arms—to prayers!" The adjutant then read a prayer of some length, and the command was given to break up the ranks.

After the review, the King invited me to walk into his house. It is a large cabin, having in the interior a certain appearance of neatness and even of luxury. It consisted of a large saloon and three chambers—calico curtains composing the partitions. The frame, made of a black hard wood, was held together by braided cords of different colors. Very fine mats covered the floor. At each end and in the side were large doors with glass windows inserted. The wall was ornamented by a number of paintings, among which I observed the portrait of King Leopold, then Duke of Saxe-Coburg, the portrait of Canning, and those of Rihoriho and his wife, painted in England. A number of chandeliers were suspended from the beams. Chairs, tables, and two or three sofas, completed the furniture. Kauikeaouli invited me to enter the interior apartments. One of them contained a magnificent estrade, fifteen feet long and eight or ten wide. This estrade or bed, raised two feet from the floor, was composed of mats, spread one upon another, in the manner already described. At the other end of the room was a bureau, upon which were some loose papers and a small book-case containing some religious books, which probably, are not often read by the King, and a history of France presented him some days before by an officer of the *Bonite*, and which he will not read oftener than his other books, although he expressed to us a strong desire to learn the French language.

This house is situated at the extremity of an extensive court, surrounded, as are all the houses of this country, by a wall of bricks dried in the sun. In this enclosure are nearly fifty huts, which serve for kitchens, store-houses, lodgings for the King's servants, and barracks for the soldiers.

Kauikeaouli improves surprisingly upon acquaintance. He is naturally timid, but if he discovers kindness and indulgence in the person with whom he enters into conversation, he becomes confiding, and then can be perceived in him the germ of an understanding which needs only to be developed. He asks many questions, and sometimes the answers call forth from him very judicious reflections. He appears to have a vivid perception of his own ignorance, although his character is naturally fickle and inconstant. But these defects result, without doubt, from the education he has received, and his ideas, constantly directed to frivolous occupations, have little to do with serious subjects. The society also in which he mingles, tends not a little to confirm the habits of dissipation which he contracted in his childhood, and he delivers himself up, with deplorable readiness, to the influence of evil examples. He received one day, while on board a whaling ship, a decided taste for pugilistic combats, and for a long time the recreation of the King and of the young people of his court, consisted in boxing; and this pastime was in vogue on our arrival. Then we were called upon to furnish amusement. In his visits aboard the *Bonite* he had occasion to see our men go through the exercise of fencing, and no persuasion was needed to turn his thoughts to this new distraction. During the whole time of our stay he was constantly fencing, either with the men, whom at his request the commandant sent to him, or with those of our sailors who passed near his house. He stopped them, brought them in and then laying aside the royal dignity together with his coat, he feared no loss of reputation from crossing swords with them during entire hours.

Thus giving himself up entirely to his capricious passions, he relinquishes the care of government to his sister-in-law, Kinau. She, as I have already remarked, is completely under the influence of the missionaries, and they govern in her name. The missionaries, however, are not certain of the duration of their domination, and the opposition which is excited against them among the foreigners fails not to trouble them. The King and his court are in open enmity with them. It is with reluctance that the King submits outwardly to their religious and police regulations, and often does he shake off this yoke; but his desires for independence reach not to the determination of seeing clearly into the affairs of state, and it is his personal conduct only that he strives to withdraw from the investigation and the censure of the missionaries. Thus there exists at present, a sort of tacit compact between the missionaries and himself; an agreement, so to speak, has been entered into between them, that he will not interfere with the government, on condition that no evangelical censure shall ever cross the threshold of his palace. In consequence, Kauikeaouli spends all his evenings in a public billiard room, playing and drinking with the first one that comes; and yet, only a good occasion is needed, I believe, to elicit from this diamond, unpolished though it be, some rays of light.

We were able to perceive something of the antipathy which the King has conceived against the missionaries, at the time of our feast at the Pali. A missionary and his wife, on their way from another part of the island to Honolulu, reached the Pali at the moment when we were about to take our places at table. He barely saluted them, and then turned his back. At the same time it was remarked that the King appeared somewhat embarrassed, for a luau had always been, up to that time, a scene of debauchery, and that which was given in honor of us, was perhaps the first at which a majority of the guests did not become completely intoxicated. When the missionary went on his way and disappeared behind the first angle of the mountain, the King seemed relieved of a great burden and his natural gaity returned.

—

The Sandwich Islands are eleven in number; five of which are large, namely: Hawaii, Maui, Molokai, Oahu, and Kauai—three are small, Kahoolawe, Lanai, and Niihau; and three are islets or rocks. They are situated between the 19th and 23rd degrees of north latitude, and between the 157th and 159th degrees of west longitude.

A hasty glance at these Islands shows that they

have not figured long upon the surface of the earth. The volcanic eruptions which have produced them, are yet recent, and many promontories, upon which villages are now seen, have been formed within the memory of man. On going into the interior of the Islands, the truth of this assertion becomes evident. We can follow, step by step, the march of creation and take her, so to speak, in the very act. It is easy to distinguish, as one ascends, the modifications through which the lava must have passed in order to be decomposed and become vegetable earth. Thus the lava which formed the lower points with which the shore is, as it were, indented, is still almost everywhere such as the volcano threw it out; yet the natural and artificial irrigations and the heat of the climate have already in some valleys near the shore, and especially on Oahu, decomposed the lava on the surface, and have rendered it capable of producing certain plants with short roots, without being able to nourish vigorous trees; and no sooner do the roots penetrate to the lava, than the plant dries up and dies. I remarked in our excursion to the Pali, that all of the trees which had reached the height of ten or twelve feet, were dead, while the bushes beneath them formed a thicket so dense that a man could not penetrate it. At a certain elevation the conditions necessary to the decomposition of the lava are found united with greater power than in the lower lands; the work had advanced more rapidly and the trees are much more vigorous.

Oahu, justly called the garden of the Sandwich

Islands, on account of the numerous streams which water it, is capable of recompensing the labors of agriculture with all the products of those of our colonies which are the most favored by nature. The plains of the interior and those near the shore, are exceedingly well adapted to the cultivation of sugar cane, which grows here to an astonishing size. The hills produce cotton and coffee in abundance, which can safely challenge a comparison with the most commended of similar articles. I have seen specimens of Oahu cotton which seemed to me to have a very fine and very long silk. Indigo grows spontaneously, and the high mountains offer the precious sandalwood for exportation. All the farinaceous plants, the potato, sweet potato and taro, are produced easily and in abundance. Almost all the islands in the group present the same conditions of prosperity; all are watered more or less abundantly, and wherever nature does not perform this work, industry can find the means of irrigating. The heat at the Sandwich Islands varies from sixty to eighty-four degrees of Fahrenheit. The climate is very salubrious, and epidemic diseases are as yet unknown. Rains are abundant on the coast during the months of February, March, August and September; in the mountains it rains almost incessantly. The clouds with which their summits are continually crowned are dissolved in abundant rains, which form streams, and these flow on to enrich the plains, so that nature, after having in her convulsions produced this land, labors constantly to render it fertile.

CHAPTER SEVEN

The natives of the Sandwich Islands have understood for a long time the art of irrigation. The early navigators admired their ingenious system, and there has been no change in it since. Taro, which constitutes the principal food of the inhabitants, requires at certain intervals and for certain times, to have its roots covered with water, and this operation must be repeated a great number of times before the plant reaches maturity. Taking advantage of the slope of the land, each landholder forms his own portion into terraces, separated by embankments of earth about two feet high and covered with grass. The water, let from the stream by a canal, is introduced into the upper terrace, and having flowed into that as long as necessary, it passes on to the next, and so of all. Each patch in turn is designed to sustain a family for a longer or shorter time. Thus the same water irrigates different patches, which are so planned that the taro in one patch is in full maturity when the products of the one immediately above it are exhausted.

Water at the Sandwich Islands, however, as in all other countries which produce by irrigation, is the occasion of many quarrels and sometimes of fatal accidents. It is not necessary to state that the lands of the King and of the Chiefs share the streams the most abundantly, but as there is generally a full supply of water, there is enough for each one. The harvest never fails—the cultivator is always sure of receiving the reward of his labor. It is true that a drought of a few months continuance would be sufficient, in many localities, to cause a famine; but there is no account of such a calamity, and the Sandwich Islands are so situated as to banish all fear in this respect. In like manner, the harvests are not exposed to the ravages made by rats, birds, and noxious animals, which are so troublesome in our colonies. These are presents which civilization has not yet made to this country; although it has already introduced mosquitoes, centipedes, scorpions, etc. Previous to 1822, mosquitoes were unknown at the Sandwich Islands—it would seem that they were brought from California. The same is true of centipedes and scorpions, the first of which appeared in 1829. At present these vexatious creatures especially the mosquitoes, are exceedingly multiplied, and the

Sandwich Islands yield not in this respect, to the countries where they originated.

Different kinds of domestic animals have not yet had time to multiply at these islands. Perhaps it is but a few centuries since plants began to thrust their roots across the crevices of lava rocks. For a long time the Sandwich Islands may have been only an assemblage of craters vomiting torrents of lava, which cooled in the sea and thus enlarged the base of the volcano. Then, when this land was formed, when it had become habitable and fertile, Nature took care to cause nutritious plants to spring up, to people it with birds, and to send inhabitants. But she was doubtless interrupted before she had completed her task; for Cook found only a few quadrupeds, very few insects, and some birds (at the present time there are only ten or twelve species). The population were long under the necessity of subsisting on fruit and fish, as the dog, the only quadruped on the islands, was reserved exclusively for the chiefs, being eaten by them only on great occasions.

Many theories have been advanced as to the manner in which the Sandwich and other islands of the Pacific were peopled, and each theory has been supported by arguments more or less weighty. I make no pretensions to have solved a problem which has baffled perhaps the researches of many who were in a far better situation than myself to discover the truth, yet I have been induced to embrace the opinion of European residents, a class by no means well instructed it is true, but serious observers. They believe that all the islands of the ocean between the tropics, were first peopled by Malays, who were driven upon these shores by the winds, and they support their opinion by the following facts:

In 1822 or 1823, a Japanese junk was cast upon the shores of Maui. There were seventeen men on board, and they had been eleven months at sea and had lost many of their companions.

In 1832, another Japanese junk arrived on the southern side of Oahu. It was navigated by four men, who were dying with hunger, and who had been obliged to take every precaution to sustain life. They stated that it was about ten moons since they left Japan, at which time their ship's company consisted of thirty-six men; that shortly after sailing they experienced a violent gale from the west, which drove them from their course, they knew not where; that at length the cold became very severe, and that they came in sight of land which was covered with snow, at which time many of their companions died with cold; that for a long time the wind drove them along the coast of this inhospitable land; that at length the wind changed and they lost sight of land; and after many moons, the weather having gradually become warmer, they came in sight, though at great distance, of land, towards which the wind was urging them; and that in this way they reached the Sandwich Islands. They stated that for a long time they had nothing to drink but rain water which they caught in their sails, and that when this failed them they drank sea water.

These facts cannot be doubted, as they have been confirmed to me by the testimony of twenty different individuals. But what causes these persons to believe that the Hawaiian people owe their origin to the Malays rather than to the Japanese, is a certain analogy in the physiognomy of the two nations, and especially the great number of Malay words found in the Hawaiian language. Mr. Reynolds, United States consul at Honolulu, assures me that the Hawaiian language contained more than two hundred Malay words. There is then a probability that one or more Malay vessels driven from their course by a strong southwest wind, would have been borne on towards the northwest coast of America; there, meeting with westerly winds, they would have been conducted to a certain longitude, and thence to one of the Pacific islands. What has happened twice in fifteen years, must, or at least may have happened in former years.

The Hawaiians are of a copper complexion; the men are generally large and well formed, with long black hair, which seldom curls. The women are smaller, and far from being so well formed as the men; yet they possess a good degree of gracefulness. As a general thing, the men wear no beard. Some are seen with naked hair, either colored with lime, as is often the case, or perhaps natural, resulting from a union of races. The chiefs seem to form a distinct class, on account of their size and stature. But this difference can only be attributed, I believe, to the life which they lead. I observed the beauty of their teeth and the smallness of their feet.

Almost all the chiefs and old men appeared to me to have conformed to the ancient custom which required men and women to knock out one or two of the front teeth on the death of a father, a mother, a friend, or a chief. I saw but very few cases of deformity; this, however, has been remarked of all savage nations. Free in their conduct and in their dress, they are not exposed to those accidents which sometimes in civilized nations are followed with such fearful consequences for infants.

In disposition the natives are mild, timid, cheerful, acute, and observing. They are generally much given to laughter. When we were lying at anchor at Kealakeakua, the noise which they made around the ship reminded me of the tumults which I have often heard in the South American forests when all the trees were covered with a host of macaws and parrots; yet they seemed more grave and less loquacious when I visited them on shore.

I remarked that a happy change has been wrought in the character of this people. Cook represents them as very adroit thieves, and he speaks of the many precautions, almost always useless, which he was obliged to take in order to protect from their covetousness the articles which might be stolen. We were informed, and our own experience confirmed the truth of the information, that no traces of this thievish disposition remain. Not an article of ours was stolen, and yet the natives had a thousand opportunies of stealing. At the time of our excursion at Kealakeakua, we got wet in landing, and spread our soaked garments upon the sand. When we gathered them up, not an article was missing; yet a hun-

dred natives, men and women, were around us, and
there were many things calculated to tempt them. I
happened to drop a silver buckle in the sand, without
perceiving it, and an Indian who had found it came on a
run to bring it to me.

Each family lives in its own house and cultivates
its own field of taro; the women share the cares of agriculture with the men, prepare the food of the family,
and make cloth for its garments. The men spend the
most of their time in fishing and in procuring shells
which they dispose of to ships. The people are called
out on certain days, to cultivate the lands of the king
and chiefs; on those days the canoes are *tabu,* and on
the previous evening they are drawn ashore, and the bay
is deserted. These employments however, are far from
occupying all their time, especially in those islands
where civilization has not created new wants. Whenever
we went ashore, a crowd of men and women followed
us in our excursions, during entire days. The women, as
we observed, spend three or four hours a day in playing
in the waves. This is almost the only amusement in
which I have seen them engage. Formerly the song and
the dance caused the hours of leisure to pass pleasantly;
but now that these pleasures are forbidden, I know not
how this people employ themselves when they have
nothing to do. I imagine that in a civilized country, one
may rigorously abstain from the dance and the song,
for visits, conversations, shows, and a thousand subjects of distraction, cause time to pass rapidly; but what
would one have these poor savages do, for savages they

still are, if those pleasures to which they are habituated are to be prohibited them, before they are put in a condition to invent for themselves others more rational and perhaps less innocent? Besides, the facility with which the missionaries have brought this people to support their influence, although at times a little tyrannical, proves how easy it is to govern them, and how few efforts would be necessary to lead them to the end which they have doubtless proposed.

All the navigators who have visited the Sandwich Islands have given some account of the religion of the islanders; it would be useless to repeat what they have said. Besides, my object being simply to make known this people such as they are at the present time, and the changes brought about by the contact of civilized nations, I shall content myself by sketching the principal features of their ancient religion. Every thing which inspired them with fear, the islanders imagined to be a god; these were monstrous divinities, to whom they sacrificed human victims on certain occasions, either to render them propitious when commencing a campaign, or when chiefs were sick, to exorcise the god of death. It was often the case also, that numerous victims accompanied the chiefs to the tomb, and these were selected from their most intimate servants.

On Hawaii, Pele, the goddess of volcanos, while she constantly threatened the life and property of the natives, received many sacrifices from them. When there was an earthquake, when large pillars of smoke rose above the clouds, when at night columns of flame darting from the sides of the mountain, painted the sky with a blood red color, they then sent victims to Pele, to mitigate her anger; but, alas! the goddess was inexorable. She accomplished by means of her ravages, the work of creation, which a god more powerful than herself had imposed on her. She added a new stratum of lava to those of which this land is formed.

The god of Oahu had also the reputation of being very powerful; he was, moreover, a very great eater. The richest offerings of taro and sweet potatoes scarcely satisfied him, and always, by means of his priests, his appetite demanded numerous contributions from the harvests of the faithful. This god was also of colossal stature, and much benefit did he derive from it. It once happened that the sun did not appear at Oahu. The men were sad; many of them became fools, and terrible diseases decimated the population. Numerous victims were sacrificed to the god, and during two moons, the whole island lay prostrate before his altars. The king of a great country towards the south (Tahiti without doubt), had taken the sun prisoner, thrust him into a very deep cavern, and closed up the entrance with immense blocks of lava. Nor did his precautions end here; he had placed at the entrance as sentinel a bird which uttered a piercing cry whenever he heard the least noise; and at the head of his intrepid warriors he was always ready to rush upon those who should dare attempt the release of the prisoner. But all this did not intimidate the powerful god of Oahu, who had been moved by the groans of his worshipers. He was a very great god.

When he went from one island to another, the water reached only to his ankles; and it came up only to his knees, when he went to the country of the south. It was night when he arrived at Tahiti. He advanced so softly that the bird did not hear him, and he strangled him before he could utter a cry; then removing with his powerful hands the blocks which closed up the entrance of the cavern, he seized the sun and hurled him into the air with incredible force. When he was at a certain distance from the shore, he raised a shout, which awoke the king of Tahiti and his warriors; they ran to the cavern, but their astonishment was great when they perceived that the sun had been rescued. The god of Oahu had hurled him to so great a height that they were never able to take him again. Since that time, the sun has always shone at Oahu.

Each of the gods had his priests, whose wants were abundantly supplied from the altar; their influence was very great, and they often held, it is said, the destinies of chiefs and kings in their hands. Kamehameha took upon himself the whole spiritual authority, being at the same time both conqueror and sovereign pontiff. He well knew the influence which this union of power gave him, and never could the efforts of missionaries, who arrived from the United States a short time before his death, obtain permission from him to aim a single blow at the religious belief of the country. "Your religion," said he, when the subject was introduced, "is perhaps very good for your nation; but the gods of Hawaii are indispensable to the Hawaiian nation. They gave me the strength to conquer; they gave me power to reign. I know not your god; why should I forsake mine?" For a savage, Kamehameha was a shrewd politician. He well understood how much influence religion must have over the people which he governed. This power was in his own hands, and he knew that it would pass into the hands of the men who should give to the nation a new god, whose priests they themselves would be; yet he mitigated some of the rigors of the tabu.

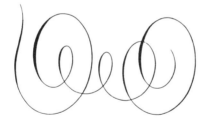

View of Honolulu

Lauvergne

CHAPTER EIGHT

The *tabu,* which I have often mentioned, was a prohibition, sometimes religious, sometimes civil, of the use of certain things. They were even forbidden to touch, or look at them. Tabu was either temporary, or permanent. The permanent or sacred tabu was inherent in the thing declared tabu. Thus, the person of the king and of the priests, the house of the king, the place where he bathed, the temples, the offerings made to the gods, and the royal sepulchres were always tabu. By degrees the priests and chiefs extended the tabu and made a speculation of it. Certain kinds of feathers and of fishes became tabu to the people; only the king and principal chiefs could wear those feathers and eat those fishes. The infraction of the permanent tabu was almost always punished with death; very severe corporal punishment was inflicted upon those who violated the temporal tabu.

The priests sometimes pronounced a general tabu upon the whole country, sometimes on a village, and sometimes, upon a single house. Now one thing was interdicted by the tabu; and then another. In certain cases, the tabu forbade the lighting of kukui-nut torches, the eating of fish and of cocoa-nuts, fishing, going out of the houses &c. In other cases, it was a means of appropriating to the exclusive use of the priests and chiefs an article which had become rare. And often, the sole object of it was to exhibit the power of the priests to the minds of the people, by making them experience it, even in their own houses. The tabu then may be considered as a means, employed by the most powerful, to impose their will upon the most feeble. From the chiefs it descended to the other classes; the men had made a thousand things tabu to the women, among which things were cocoa-nuts, certain kinds of fish, and bananas; neither were they permitted to stop in the apartment where the men took their food.

Kamehameha, as I have stated, diminished the severity of the penalty for breaking the tabu; but it was not till the reign of Rihoriho, that the tabu was entirely abolished. The women especially, and the people experienced the benefits of this religious reform, which must be ascribed to the influence exerted by the American missionaries upon the minds of the chiefs. Yet a cry of horror arose in all the islands, when the high priest proclaimed the tabu abolished; but this people, so mild and so easily governed, very soon forgot their wooden gods; they destroyed the idols to which they had so long sacrificed human victims, and, following the example of the chiefs, they prostrated themselves in crowds before the altars of the new religion. The regent, Kaahumanu, was one of the first to embrace Christianity, and she gave all her influence to the efforts put forth by the missionaries to establish and spread the Christian religion.

A little later, in 1827 I believe, two Catholic missionaries, Messrs. Bachelot and Short, arrived at Honolulu; they established themselves there at first without opposition, and, as all the inhabitants testify, their public and private conduct was always exemplary. Mild, affable, humble, devoting themselves without ambition, and without selfishness to their work of regeneration, they soon made a great number of proselytes. Then the Protestant missionaries began to believe that the competition of the Catholic missionaries would become dangerous, and they took measures to arrest it. One day in 1832, the two missionaries were dragged from their residence by order of Kaahumanu, put on board a Hawaiian vessel, and, after a month's voyage during which they suffered the greatest privations, they were landed on the coast of California, forty miles from any habitation, without food, without water, and without arms to defend themselves against the wild beasts.

The French government were never, I think, made acquainted with this affair, which demanded, perhaps, its intervention. These meek and peaceful men were

doubtless unwilling to draw the severity of our government upon this country. They might also, without
sufficient reason, have believed that after the revolution
of July, two poor, persecuted missionaries would not be
believed. If such was their belief, they were in error,
and the protection of France would certainly not have
been withheld from them, if the matter had come to the
knowledge of the government; they will find evidence of
this in the measures which will doubtless be taken to
prevent a recurrence of similar acts.* The present is not
a period of religious persecutions. I have been assured
that the order for the embarkation (of the two Catholic
priests) and the arrangements which accompanied it
were written entirely by the hand of a missionary
known at Honolulu. I can hardly believe, notwithstanding, that in the nineteenth century, men belonging
to a free and enlightened nation could resolve to give
such an example of persecution and intolerance. Messrs.
Bachelot and Short are still in California, as I have been
informed.

The alarm felt in Honolulu on the arrival of the
Bonite was from the fear that she had come to demand
satisfaction for this injustice. Mr. Walch, an Irish
Catholic missionary, had arrived a few days before and
received a verbal order to depart immediately; but in

---

*The following note appeared in the original French version.
Since this account was written, the French government have sent a frigate
to the Sandwich Islands; the commandant of the ship has taken evidence,
upon the spot, of this scandalous abuse of power, and there is every reason
to believe that for the future, the character of French and Catholic will not
be a cause of oppression in these islands.

accordance with the advice of the English consul, he had refused to obey unless he should receive a written order. This order was to be sent him the day that we arrived; but the presence of the *Bonite*, doubtless, produced a change in the intentions of Kinau. The order was not sent, and sixteen days after, at the time of our departure, Mr. Walch had not only not received it, but there had been nothing more said to him about leaving. As an English sloop-of-war, the *Acteon*, arrived at Honolulu the day that we sailed, it is not probable that Mr. Walch will experience any further molestation. But the proselytes made by the two Catholic missionaries were cruelly persecuted. All who would not abjure the Catholic faith were cast into prison and sentenced to the basest labors. Some of them are still groaning in dungeons.

When mention was made to the king of the violence enacted against the Catholic missionaries, he replied that this act had taken place under the regency of Kaahumanu, that he had nothing at all to do with it, and that, consequently, he could not be held responsible. He furthermore added that he was aware of the fact that almost all the wars which had disquieted the states of Europe were occasioned by the co-existence of two rival religions. The Presbyterian religion having first been taught on the Sandwich Islands, another religion, he said, could not be admitted; and it was only in this way that he could preseve tranquility among his people; one religion was abundantly sufficient for 100,000 or 150,000 inhabitants. Kauikeaouli, in speaking thus, gave evidence of great wisdom; and moreover, of a knowledge of history which I should not have suspected. I cordially approve of the principle advocated by the king; but those who taught him so fine a sentiment should have added that in the United States there is a greater variety of religious opinions perhaps than in any other country; that the Catholics are not persecuted there; and that the nation is not, on account of religion, desolated with civil war; that intolerance is the primary cause of disorders; and that in violating the individual liberty of the Catholic missionaries, and in banishing them by an arbitrary act, Kaahumanu perpetrated a deed of hateful intolerance.

At the present time, the Presbyterian religion is spread over all the Sandwich Islands, that is, the natives, on the sabbath, attend religious worship in the churches of the Presbyterian missionaries; but unfortunately, with very few exceptions, this conversion is almost always entirely nominal. Indeed, the natives are not yet in a condition to understand their new religion; moreover, it is presented to them under an aspect too severe and mystical. In all places at a distance from the residence of the missionaries, the islanders have preserved, if not the barbarous customs of their old religion, at least their absurd superstitions. The work is then only commenced; but the force of circumstances, in spite of the system pursued by the missionaries, will work out for this people those moral and physical improvements, which a better management would have secured much sooner.

The missionaries of the different islands assemble every year at Honolulu; a schooner which belongs to the mission goes for them to their different places of residence. This is a sort of annual council where each one reports the results of his labors during the year, and where they concert measures for the future. All the missionaries of the Sandwich Islands are Americans, as all those of the Society Islands are English. It is by a kind of tacit agreement that the clergy of these two nations have divided the spiritual domination, and I am almost ready to add, the temporal also, of the islands of the Pacific.

Lahaina on the Island of Maui may be considered as the capital of the mission. It is there that the missionaries have their principal establishment and their high school, a sort of nursery where are trained the monitors who are to assist the missionaries in their labors.

There is a printing office at Lahaina and two at Honolulu, one of which belongs to the mission and the other, to the editor of a newspaper published in English and called *The Sandwich Island Gazette*. The *Gazette* is a weekly paper, edited by an American, and opposed to the missionaries. The *Ke Kumu* (flambeau, professor), a newspaper published in Hawaiian by the missionaries, contains nothing but the notices of the arrival and sailing of vessels, and extracts from religious works. I observed that among the very great number of books printed in Hawaiian, very few had reference to the progress of industry, or of science;

all, with the exception of a few elementary works of arithmetic and geography, were on religious subjects, such as commentaries on the Bible, catechisms for the use of the natives, or hymn books. I do not, by any means, deny the utility of these works, nor their indispensable necessity even; but I can give no reason why the missionaries, always so zealous and persevering in their religious duties, have altogether neglected to impart to the islanders any notions of industry, of the mechanic arts, of manufactures, and of agriculture; notions, without which, the natives can derive no advantage from civilization. I testified my surprise that I had not found any knowledge of history among the chiefs, and the answer was made that in reading the history of other nations, the natives would only learn too soon to be corrupt and perverse; that it would be better for civilization to enter the country by a purer medium, and that those who had charge of the mission would know when it would be a suitable time to make known to the inhabitants of the Sandwich Islands the history of the nations of the old world, taking care to prune off everything having a tendency to awaken polluting ideas in the readers. In the meantime, this people coming in daily contact with runaway sailors and with vagrants, and who see, with but very few exceptions, only the refuse of society, are becoming contaminated by this ruinous intercourse without being able to oppose to the evil the natural defence which is found in the occupations of industry and in a more enlarged and liberal education.

The best means of rendering the new religion dear to this people would have been to demonstrate to them that their present condition could only be improved by the change; but they have experienced, even to this day only the privations and the sternness of the religion which has been imposed upon them. It has subjected them to a life to which they were not accustomed; it demands a large part of the time which they are able to devote to labor; it forbids their engaging in the sports and amusements to which they were attached; and as an offset, it offers them nothing but purely metaphysical advantages which they can neither appreciate nor conceive of.

Moreover, this people, which early navigators represented as so happy in their nakedness, seemed to us to be miserable under the rags with which civilization has covered them. What then has been gained by the change? When Cook discovered the Sandwich Islands he found the inhabitants cheerful and happy. Their enjoyment was material, it is true; with mental pleasures they were unacquainted. Living with scarcely the least reference to the future, they were not even conscious of their dignity as men.

They have been deprived of their sensual enjoyments, and mental pleasures have not been furnished for them. I know that civilization always commences in this way, and that it must destroy barbarism in order to create upon its ruins. But has all been done that ought to be done? Has the path, pointed out by reason, humanity, and even by the interests of religion, been pursued? Surely not; and where it has not, the natives will be found to regret their ancient customs and to undervalue the benefits of civilization. It was not requisite that they should hear the mystic language of the Bible; their minds were not sufficiently mature to comprehend these sublime truths. It was enough for them to learn the fundamental doctrines of the Christian religion, those simple and pure doctrines which they could easily understand. It was necessary to put forth efforts for the physical well-being of the people, to enjoy speedily the fruits of that civilization which has been brought to them. The missionaries would have been able to use their unlimited influence in order to do away with those despotic institutions which give up the fortunes of the natives to the caprice of a chief, and to replace them by wise and liberal laws. How could the citizens of a free people suffer such abuses to exist? Were they afraid of going too far and of compromising their influence? They have, forsooth, managed this people as they pleased. They have taken from them their costume, their habits and religion. They have seen the high priest himself proclaiming the weakness of the gods and, at their word, applying the torch to those temples and idols by which he governed the people; and they have been afraid to meddle with the absurd laws which were enacted in times of despotism and barbarism; in times, however, when the caprice and cupidity of the chiefs being necessarily limited, those laws were far less oppressive than at present. Verily the system pursued in the Sandwich Islands cannot be too severely condemned, when the consequences are considered.

In fine, although the property of the citizen should be made inviolable; although just bounds should be placed to the despotism of the chiefs, yet, at the same time, the development of commerce, of industry, and of agriculture ought to be patronized in every possible way; and to accomplish this foreigners ought to be invited in and encouraged. To throw obstacle upon obstacle in the way of their establishment in the country, as has been done, was not sound policy.

But, the objection will be made, *it is foreigners that have corrupted the native population.* I admit it, and that was the first effect that the contact of civilization ought to produce. It was an inevitable evil; but the only possible remedy should have been applied, and in the very cause of the evil the remedy was to be found. You should either have left this savage people as you found them and withdrawn from them; or else you should have drawn them away from the pernicious influence of the only European society known to them; and the settlement in the country of industrious foreigners, merchants, agriculturists, &c., could only bring about this result. Is it to be believed that savages can take examples in morals from the sailors of whale ships?

Valley of the Pali near Honolulu   *Fisquet*

CHAPTER NINE

The missionaries found this people without a character, with vices which were only superficial, with simple and artless manners, and with astonishing readiness to receive new impressions. And what have they done for them? They believe they have corrected their morals; but demoralization is at its height, demoralization by calculation, much more hateful than that over which they claim the merit to have triumphed. They believe they have made Christians, but they have made hypocrites only. They believe they have ameliorated the physical condition of the people; but they have made them acquainted with misery which they did not know.

Still it is an incontrovertible truth, that the missionaries have done much for the tribes of the ocean; but they have imposed far too narrow limits upon their mission, they are far from having done all the good which they might have done. To what ought this to be ascribed? Perhaps to an excess of zeal; perhaps also to the education not sufficiently liberal which they have received. Imbued with a religious sternness so remarkable in certain sects, they have lost sight of the temporal good of this people in their effort to make them participate in those spiritual treasures which they esteem above all things. They have abolished barbarous and revolting practices for the sake of humanity, and they have given the natives some ideas of civilized society; but having reached the point when reform would produce useful results, they stopped short. It might be said that they have been constantly under the influence of interested considerations. Thus they have established schools, but they have proscribed the study of the English language. What could have been their object in this? They evidently feared, as I have already stated, that the influence of the European residents would counter-balance their own. But this was not the greatest obstacle to the progress of civilization; and is there not evidently an anomaly between the end proposed and the means employed? Have the missionaries wished, by rendering the intercourse between the natives and foreigners more difficult, to arrest the contagion of vice? But all the world knows, and at the Sandwich Islands the fact is more evident than elsewhere, that vice needs no language in order to have intercourse; example alone, has been sufficient to corrupt this people, so artless and susceptible.

Since the discovery of these islands their population have decreased in a fearful manner. It is already reduced to one-fourth, at least, of what it was at the time of Cook's first voyage. This diminution is ascribed to different causes. Strong drink has been here, as among all savage nations, a poison brought by Europeans. Diseases unknown in former times have infected the nation. Licentiousness has been followed with consequences so much the more terrible in this country, as the contagion spread everywhere, without the least resistance, for it was an unknown evil. One cause of depopulation as potent, at least, as licentiousness, still exists in a disease mentioned by many European physicians, who have been established for a long time at Honolulu. This disease, which was introduced about ten years ago, attacks women in childbed, and proves fatal in three cases out of five. At first white pimples appear on the lips, and these extend by degrees to the throat, the stomach, the bowels. It generally commences eight or ten days before confinement, and ends almost always in the death of both mother and child. But whatever may be the causes which are decimating the population of the Sandwich Islands, is it not lamentable and surprising that wherever civilization has come in contact with the savage state, this contact has been fatal to the people it ought to regenerate? The effects are everywhere the same, though the causes may be different. Fanatical and sanguinary in Mexico and Peru, encroaching in the United States, religious and mystical in the Sandwich Islands; into whatever country civilization has penetrated, there have the aborigines disappeared before it. What have become of the people that once covered the valleys of Spanish America? Civilization has destroyed them. At the present time you will scarcely find any vestiges of them in the lowest classes of society. What remains in the valleys of the Ohio, the Missouri and the Mississippi, of the numerous tribes that once roamed through the forests? The vicinity of the whites has caused them to disappear, and soon the inquiry will be made if these nations even existed. The population will melt away before civilized man, either by this terrible mortality which is consuming it, or because it will mingle and lose itself in the migrations from Europe and America. And this intermingling should be encouraged by all possible means; and to this end wise laws should be enacted, industry should be called in, agriculture encouraged, and commerce patronized. These are the means by which these wretched people can be saved from a state of decay which is paralyzing its vital principles. Unless haste is made, there will be none left at the Sandwich Islands to civilize, unless it be the civilizers themselves.

The government of the Sandwich Islands is monarchical and absolute; but it has undergone important modifications since the discovery of the island. Formerly each island of the group was governed by a chief who was independent of his neighbours. These sovereigns were engaged in war the most part of the time. At

length Kamehameha, heir to the sovereignty of the
Island of Hawaii, began that series of conquests that
rendered him absolute king of all the islands.

Kamehameha possessed superior talents for observation, and his perseverance was remarkable. He quick-
ly perceived what powerful assistance he might derive
from Europeans, who at that time began to visit these
islands, and his first care was to attach a large number
of them to his service. At his death, which took place
in 1819, his son Rihoriho ascended the throne. Some
manifestations of insurrection appeared on Kauai, but
they were immediately suppressed by Rihoriho who
with a single devoted companion crossed the sea to find
his rival. He, filled with admiration for such a noble
manifestation of confidence, acknowledged him as his
sovereign. It was Rihoriho who abolished the ancient
worship which Kamehameha, either from conviction or
political considerations, wished to remain unimpaired.
Rihoriho likewise abolished the tabu. At this period
the influence of the missionaries began to be in the
ascendant. This ascendancy became unbounded on the
death of Rihoriho, who in 1824 went to die in England.
Kaahumanu, widow of Kamehameha, and regent during
the minority of Kauikeaouli, displayed a zeal which
approached even to fanaticism in the practice of her
new religion, and she gave herself up entirely to the
guidance of the missionaries.

On the death of Kaahumanu, Kinau, her daughter
succeeded her in the regency, ruled by the same ascendancy, blindly adopted all the measures which were

dictated to her by the mission, and the authority of the missionaries gave law to the country. To this system no change was made, as I have already stated, when Kauikeaouli became of age. Accustomed to yield to the will of his sister he has not to this day performed an act of authority. Yet his well known aversion to innovation, and some supposed tendency in him to independence, gave rise to a plan among the chiefs of the regent's party, of removing him to Maui, which was the most devoted of all the islands of the group, to the new system. Kauikeaouli was made acquainted with this project by the almost simultaneous departure of all his servants. In this crisis he applied to the foreign residents of Honolulu, who promised to stand by him; and their firmness, well known to the opposite party, caused the failure of the project. Kauikeaouli can find out whenever he pleases, and shall know how to employ it, how great are the elements of power in the support which foreigners will lend him. This occurred in 1832. At this time there appeared two documents or proclamations, one from Kinau, and the other from Kauikeaouli, who then attained to his majority. These two documents, published in Hawaiian, professed to set forth their respective rights, but on the part of the king it was a vain form, and he soon fell again under the yoke of his sister.

Soon after the idea was suggested to the king, by whom it is not known, of undertaking the conquest of the New Hebrides. It was his design, if successful, to abandon the Sandwich Islands with all his court, and to found a new kingdom in the conquered country. Two brigs were employed in this expedition, and the command devolved upon Boki,* one of the generals of Kamehameha, and Governor of Oahu; but never did enterprize terminate more unfortunately. The brig, on board of which Boki embarked, was driven off by a southerly gale, and was never heard of after. The crew of the other brig, *Harrietta,* to the number of more than a hundred men, all perished of an epidemic before reaching their destination. It was necessary to send a new crew from Honolulu, to take back the brig from Viti, or Fiji, where it had been abandoned.

At the present time affairs are almost in the same condition as in 1832. Kauikeaouli evidently seeks to shut his eyes to the state of dependence in which his sister holds him; and while he delivers himself up to the dissipation of a life entirely sensual, Kinau governs or rather the missionaries in her name.

But the machinery of the government is very simple. The king issues his orders and the subjects obey. There is no necessity that the laws of the sovereign be accompanied by commentaries. At present this absolute power is modified in only a very slight degree by the influence of the missionaries, who are more interested in the propagation of their religion than in the temporal

---

Note written by the Editor of THE FRIEND, October 1, 1850.
*Boki's expedition consisting of the brigs Kamehameha and Becket, sailed December 2nd, 1829, and not in 1832 as stated above. It was Boki's expedition, not the King's; the object was to procure sandalwood, not to found a new kingdom. The King objected to Boki's going in person, even after he had gone on board to sail.

welfare of the people. The regulations introduced by them are exclusively religious; yet they have constantly opposed every measure, which by giving security to foreigners, could induce them to form any considerable commercial and agricultural establishments in this country.

Under the king, governors administer the affairs of the different islands. They are high and powerful lords, subject in name only to the authority of the sovereign, on whose account they collect the poll-tax; but only a small proportion of the value received ever finds its way to Honolulu. It would be difficult perhaps to obtain correct returns. Kuakini, for example, is as potent throughout the island of Hawaii as Kauikeaouli himself; yet the royal authority is everywhere recognized. Forty years ago the powerful Kamehameha put down all ideas of independence that could threaten the security of his crown; and now, the union of the missionaries, and their cooperation in all the measures necessary to perpetuate this unity of power, tend to the same result. There is little probability then, that any revolution will soon take place to change the form of government. It is, however, easy to foresee the result of the struggle now in progress between the missionaries and the European residents. Whatever efforts the former may make to put off the time, the day will come, I doubt not, when the number of foreigners increasing as the resources of the country increase, will paralyze all the measures of the missionaries and open these islands to a more enlarged and productive system of administration.

I will add a few words concerning the laws of the Sandwich Islands, and the administration of justice. The Hawaiian code contains ten articles. It is a sort of commentary on the decalogue, or rather the law of nature, amplified and disfigured by civilization. Every crime is punished by imprisonment, for a shorter or longer time, or by involuntary labor, but there is no one who cannot be bought off by a sum of money. Premeditated murder is the only crime that does not admit of an equivalent in money, and is punished with death; yet the premeditation can be so easily set aside that the law becomes a nullity. It demands two hundred dollars for the life of a man, and every man who can command fifty dollars may commit a rape. Hence it appears that morality is not fixed at a very high rate. In fine, the part of the code with which civilization had to do, is not the most moral.

There are three judges in Honolulu, and one judge in each district. They live on the perquisites of their office, and this is not a meager sum, for the fourth, and sometimes the third of all fines paid go to the judge. For example, if a married man commit adultery with a married woman, each must pay a fine of fifteen dollars. The man pays fifteen dollars, five to the judge, and ten to the husband of the woman. The woman pays fifteen dollars more, five to the judge, and ten to the wife of her accomplice. It is the same in civil actions. The judge receives one fourth of the value concerning which he decides.

When a foreigner commits a crime he is tried by a jury composed of an equal number of foreigners and natives. The judges have then only to enforce the law; but when a civil action comes before them, they decide according to their own judgment, and from their decision there is no appeal. It is understood that foreigners never appeal to this tribunal. All difficulties that arise among them are settled by arbitrators.

At the Sandwich Islands the people have no charter, nothing which limits the authority of the king or the chiefs. The king is absolute master of the soil, and of everything that it produces. It is only by his permission that the inhabitants live upon the land, and use the fruits of the land. Hence he has the right to dispose of everything that pertains to them. Yet, for want of written stipulations, there are certain established customs, and it is seldom that there is any departure from these. Thus, although upon the death of an occupant of a land, that land by right reverts to the king, yet he almost always permits the son of the deceased to inherit the hut and field of his father; but, I repeat, this is only a concession and not a right.

There is not at the Sandwich Islands a well established system of taxation; but it is expected that among the natives, each man pays to the king a tax of one dollar, and that each woman and each child that has attained to the height of four feet, pay half a dollar. Children whose height is less than four feet are not subject to taxation. Besides this the king receives one-half of proceeds of sales made by the natives; for example if a fowl be sold for fifty cents, one half of it, or twenty-five cents, must be paid to the king. Then two days in each week are devoted to the cultivation of the lands belonging to the king, or to the chiefs. Thus can the king call everything among this people into requisition that suits his convenience.

See what civilization has done for the people. The first care of the civilizers should have been to modify such barbarous laws.

The commerce of the Sandwich Islands is not yet of much importance. The productions of the country being of but trifling value, as a matter of course the demand for foreign goods must be unimportant. Commerce is carried on almost exclusively by American or English ships, which come directly to Honolulu, or which touch at this port either on their passage from the republics of the South Seas to China, or in going to the northwest coast of America and California. Some of these vessels dispose of their entire cargoes at Honolulu to furnish supplies for the wants for the country; or they only store them, and wait for high prices in the markets of California in order to transport them there.

A number of American houses have been established some years in Honolulu. There are four or five of them, and their business is not extensive. There is only one English house, the business transactions of which are of little importance. French commerce has appeared at the Sandwich Islands, but at long intervals. Chance only gave it this direction, and no direct operation has been undertaken in France with this country since that which was entered upon in 1826, by a house at Bordeaux, at the instigation of Rives, Kamehameha's physician, who accompanied Rihoriho to England.

Consumption at the Sandwich Islands does not amount to more than $100,000; the sum total of importations, whether for consumption or storage, scarcely amounts to $200,000.

The consumption consists of bleached and unbleached calicoes, prints, hardware, lumber, sugar, coffee, spirituous liquors, &c. The importations of articles of luxury is limited to the consumption of five or six hundred Europeans or Americans living on the different islands, and who are generally poor. The Americans bring to the islands white and unbleached cottons, soap, ready-made clothing, flour, rum, wines, and other French articles, &c. The English imports are composed principally of calicoes, white cottons, cordage, canvas, hardware, supplies for ships, &c. Lumber is brought from New Zealand, and sugar from the Society Islands or from Peru.

The Sandwich Islands furnish in exchange for these articles, provisions, sandalwood, a small quantity of kukui-nut oil, which is of an excellent quality for burning, perfectly clear and without smell, and money which they receive of the ships that touch at the islands for refreshment. But as soon as agricultural industry shall have developed the resources of the islands, they will produce all colonial commodities; and their commerce at present so limited, will increase in proportion to the increased productions of the islands. The most important commercial resource of the islands at this time is the whale ships which touch at Honolulu twice a year to repair damage and procure supplies, which are cheap and very good. Fifty or sixty American whale ships enter the port of Honolulu annually, and twenty or twenty-five English whale ships. It is calculated that the expense of each whale ship for supplies is not less than $500 each time; thus making a sum total of $35,000 or $40,000.

Sandalwood has become exceedingly scarce, so that in order to find any it is necessary to go where the country is almost impassable. During the first years of cutting sandalwood, the forests were cut down without any precaution. It was a treasure the value of which was unknown to the chiefs and abused by them when discovered. It is now almost impossible to procure a full cargo of this precious wood. If some order should be observed in cutting the trees, it might in a few years become a valuable article of export; but this cannot be hoped for. The poverty of the chiefs, joined to the passions which have been awakened in them, will prevent this; moreover they are aware that the resource is about to fail them, and they make haste to exhaust it in every possible manner.

But the greatest riches of these islands, as I have already stated, are concealed in the earth, and only the industry of Europeans and Americans can draw it forth for commerce; for the population is far from possessing the perseverance and energy which are necessary to carry on large agricultural establishments with success. If the lands remain exclusively in the hands of the natives, ages will pass before they acquire the talent or the courage to turn them to account. A people, habituated to live from hand to mouth, and almost without labor, cannot be rendered industrious at once. Up to the present time agriculture has not advanced a step, and these fertile lands are awaiting the industry which must make them productive. Each native lives in his hut, cultivates the quantity of taro which he needs, and contents himself with raising some fowls and hogs, which he sells to the ships which visit the islands; with the proceeds of these sales he pays his tax to the king, and procures for himself cloth and ardent spirits. But this resource belongs only to the aristocracy, which has already become somewhat industrious. Beneath this class is the great majority of the people, who still live as they lived before the discovery of the islands, yet with much more wretchedness, and with much higher rent to pay the chiefs.

It pertains then to the future to develop the territorial and commercial resources of the Sandwich Islands. Situated in the center of the great north Pacific Ocean, they are a sort of resting place in the midst of this vast sea, which separates India and China from America. They will acquire importance in proportion as the relation between the two continents shall be developed. Should the isthmus of Panama be opened the Sandwich Islands would of necessity become one of the most interesting places on the globe, since besides the resources which I have pointed out, they would possess the advantage of being situated on the great route between Europe and India; they would become the natural entrepot, the station-point that commerce will make for itself on this new route; to this point will center all the commerce of China, the Philippines, Chinese India, the north-west coast of America and California. Add to this advantageous situation, a fertile soil and salubrious climate, and there will be no occasion to doubt that the Sandwich Islands are destined to become a most important commercial station.

This future cannot be so far distant, as one might at first be disposed to believe. The idea of opening a canal across the isthmus of Panama is not new, and the possibility of accomplishing the project has been demonstrated more than once, whatever knowing geologists may have said about it; the supposed elevation of the Pacific above the Atlantic, which would endanger the coasts of the other continent, is a chimera; and if this fear were well founded, the difficulty of restraining the water by means of dykes, could not be compared with the obstacles to be overcome in opening the canal. Two years ago, the project of a canal proposed to the government of New Granada, a project well conceived, but unfortunately impracticable for many reasons, connected with one of the contracting parties, was accepted by that government. Immense advantages accrued to the contractor. I doubt not that it would very cheerfully accede to a proposition of the same kind, if it could only be assured of the execution of the project, by the morality and ability of the company that should undertake the magnificent enterprise. It is not long since an American company proposed to construct a railroad from Chagres to Panama; but the project of the canal came athwart this enterprise, and I know not what has become of it. But although the opening of a canal seems to me far more advantageous than the construction of a railroad, yet the latter means of conveyance would not be without an immense influence upon the condition of the Sandwich Islands; for lines of packets would doubtless be established forthwith, to ply between Panama and the various ports of the Pacific.

CHAPTER TEN

Other circumstances may attach a high degree of importance to the Sandwich Islands and render them of great consequence, as a place of refreshment to our commerce. Our commerce is banished, so to speak, from the markets of India and Indo-China, by the difficulty of procuring return cargoes for our own ships. The consumption of tea and indigo is limited in France, and a certain number of cargoes of these articles supplies our market for a long time. Besides, the profits arising from the shipping of goods to India and China cannot be sufficient to compensate our ship owners for the loss occasioned by the ships returning from so long a voyage without a cargo. Moreover, the competition of manufacturing has become so great that the nations who are sure of return cargoes to their ships

oppose to us a rivalry which we cannot withstand.
We are under the necessity, then, of proportioning the
number of ships fitted out for the East Indies to the
consumption in France of tea, indigo, and other articles brought from that part of the world. It is true
that Bourbon, and what we call *our possessions in India,*
provide us a certain amount of sugar as return cargo;
but, beyond the fact that this resource is very limited,
there is a direct commerce with Bourbon which takes
care of the exportation of the country's products; and
in any case, the freight that our China-bound ships
might pick up there is subject to uncertainties too
great for one to depend on it.†

It is evident then that, could we be assured of
return freight from India and China, we could send out
a much larger number of ships and could increase to a
considerable extent in those countries the consumption
of those articles which are in general requisition there.
Here a question is presented which has been often
agitated, and to which I shall return, as it is of vital importance to our commerce in the East, and because, in
my opinion, the interests of our manufactures have not
been appreciated to this day. I will first speak of the
admission of sugar from Manila, and Cochin China, with
duties proportioned to those which our colonial sugar
pays. When in 1817 the duties upon sugar from the
East Indies were diminished, our commerce seeing
markets opened which it had ardently desired for a long
time, it engaged with ardor in the India trade, and as
many as fifteen or twenty French ships were seen in the

bay of Manila. But this season of commercial prosperity did not continue long. The interests of our commerce, of our navigation, and of our manufactures were sacrificed, in my opinion, to interests far less important.

Often I have asked myself why France, with all her territorial resources, with the good wages of her operators, compared with the wages of operators in England, and with a thousand other causes of success, should be behind other commercial nations; why, in short, we are always the last on the ground, the gleaners, when others have gathered the harvest. When I examine with my own eyes, I am always convinced that in order to compete successfully with England and the United States, France only needs a firm determination to succeed and a rational deviation from the system which has hitherto been followed. We do not sufficiently comprehend the importance, perhaps, of a great commercial prosperity, notwithstanding our eyes have been opened for some years, and we have manifested a solicitude, which has too much respected, perhaps, those old prejudices, the pernicious influence of which seems apparent at the present time.

The English consul had the kindness to give me a list of the arrival of merchant vessels at Honolulu, the only port of the Sandwich Islands that is habitually frequented by foreign ships. This list embraces the years of 1830 to 1835, and gives a very good idea of the relations of the country; but I repeat, it would not be right to judge concerning the commercial importance which the Sandwich Islands may acquire from what they are at present. The circumstances which I have enumerated, and others besides will rapidly develop their resources, and make them, if not a considerable market, at least an important entrepot for European merchandise.

The geographic position of the Sandwich Isles calls attention to them from another point of view: situated, although at a great distance, opposite the Russian possessions of Kamstchatka, they have for a long time attracted the interest of the Russian government.† Of the eighteen vessels of war which have arrived in Honolulu since 1825, four were Russian. In case of a war between England and Russia, both these powers would, without doubt, seek to take possession of the Sandwich Islands for a military station and as a place of refuge for their ships of war and privateers.

It is true that the American influence is now dominant at the Sandwich Islands, this influence being exerted by the missionaries, all of whom came from the United States; the commerce, in like manner, is American. Yet I never would believe that England, so quick to appreciate the different military positions of the globe, and to take possession of them when they can be useful to her, has not perceived the importance of the Sandwich Islands in the event of a war between her and Russia. I never could believe that she would sleep a moment even should this danger become imminent, nor would she consent to abandon her rights to other nations when, by making sure of them in time, she could preserve an appearance of acting according to the law of nations. For a long time she has been in favorable circumstances to form an estimate of the port of Honolulu, the narrow and difficult entrance to which can be so easily defended, and which, in the hands of a hostile nation, would be the occasion of alarm to the English, for their commerce in the East. I can easily imagine that England, who regards the Sandwich Islands as having been committed to her guardianship in consequence of the cession made to Vancouver by Kamehameha, an act without validity, if you please, but which will not the less serve for a pretext, whenever England shall deem it expedient to take possession; I can easily imagine, I say, that England has not, to this day, judged it necessary to establish a garrison at Honolulu, as it would cost much money and would be entirely useless in present circumstances; but I am fully persuaded that she has her eyes constantly on the Sandwich Islands, and that she perfectly appreciates the importance of their position in case of war.

The political relations of the Sandwich Islands, with the governments of civilized nations, are limited to two acts: the first is that by which, on the 25th of February, 1794, Kamehameha acknowledged himself and his people as subjects of His Britannic Majesty.

The second political act is the Treaty of Commerce, signed on the 23rd of December, 1826, between Kauikeaouli and the government of the United States. This treaty grants no exclusive advantage to Americans; it secures to the citizens, and to the property of the citizens of the United States, the protection of the

Hawaiian government, *against all enemies* in case of war; *it sanctions the admission of American vessels into the ports of the Sandwich Islands, and gives them permission to trade with the inhabitants of the islands.* The following Articles establish certain rules for the saving of American ships that may suffer shipwreck on the coast of the Hawaiian Islands, and for the arrest of deserters. This treaty ends with the usual clause that *American commerce shall enjoy all the advantages that may be allowed to the most favored nation,* stipulating on this point, full reciprocity for the commerce of the Sandwich Islands and the United States.

The English have not wanted to make a treaty with a country, of which they regard themselves as the lords paramount; for by a treaty they would relinquish their rights in lawsuits. They have therefore abstained from every political act with the Hawaiian government. The Americans, on the contrary, foreseeing that the English will one day be able to make good that acquired right to the Sandwich Islands, desire to secure by a treaty the advantages which they now enjoy, and of which they might be deprived by another government taking possession. This treaty, therefore, should be their security. In this the Americans have been guided by a wise foresight; they have perceived all the commercial importance which the Hawaiian Islands will acquire, and they have taken measures to secure their commerce in case of a revolution in the government.

Should we not profit by their example, and by a treaty secure to ourselves the advantages which the geographical position of the islands may offer to our commerce? It is true that at present a treaty of commerce with the governments of the islands in the Pacific would but slightly benefit our commercial navigation; but it would by a document, laid away in our archives until there should be occasion to use it.

The treaty between the United States and the Sandwich Islands is incomplete, and the American agent, wholly occupied with the commercial relations of his countrymen, has not fully appreciated the circumstances of the country with which he treats. He has not given attention to the establishments already formed at the Sandwich Islands by Americans, nor to those which an increase of commerce will cause to spring up. The existing establishments have been founded without precaution, each occupying a lot of land ceded by the government, say the proprietors, but without any ostensible act. Now the government, trusting to the ancient laws of the country, claims to be the exclusive proprietor of all the lands, and this claim includes those where foreigners have formed their establishments, permitting them to occupy the lots during life, but on the condition that the lots and the buildings shall revert to the Crown whenever the resident shall die or leave the country. The government has declared, moreover, that no foreigner can own lands at the Sandwich Islands, a measure which has been dictated to it, and the pernicious influence of which has not been calculated.

This declaration of the government has arrested every effort which agricultural industry might put forth at the islands, and produced a want of confidence in commerce which only tends to paralyze their progress. Foreigners who would be glad to engage in agricultural labors, requiring a great outlay of capital, are prevented by the certainty that if any malady, or any motive whatever, should induce them to leave the country, they would lose at once the fruit of their labors, that their death, moreover, would take it away from their children. Those who establish themselves in these islands, having always to take into consideration a forced abandonment at length, proportion their investments to the chances of success which an inconsiderable establishment can offer. Consequently, agriculture has made no progress, and, instead of immense establishments which a more enlarged policy would have caused to spring up, no other cultivation is seen on the fertile plains of the Sandwich Islands than that of the taro. The system pursued by the government occasions distrust; it shows that jealousy of foreigners already exists, and it bodes ill for the future.

Yet it is undoubtedly true that this country can no longer be satisfied with its ancient standing; the people have entered upon a new life; their wants are increased, and industry alone can furnish means to satisfy them. To paralyze the resources of the country would be to expose it to complete demoralization, the consequences of which are already beginning to show themselves in a fearful manner.

On the other hand, it would be unjust to demand liberty for each one to build and plant upon government lands without having previously purchased them. But what is the tendency of the system now in vogue, a system which keeps at a distance, and discourages foreign industry? Is it not to render the land almost entirely unproductive? Oahu contains a population of 20,000 (I mention this island because its population is the most dense), and taking into consideration plains, hills and mountains, it contains an area of 600 square leagues (530 square miles). A thousandth part of this, perhaps, is cultivated. Can this still savage people draw forth from this land the treasures which it contains? Will these men become the enterprising proprietors who will be able to obtain skillful planters from India and America, or from Europe, and direct them? Besides, will not this people, which has for forty years been diminishing in a fearful progression, continue to diminish from the same causes? Must it not expect the fate of all those savage tribes which the contact of civilization has smitten with death, and which have disappeared from the face of the earth before the work of regeneration was accomplished?

When we arrived at Honolulu, we found there the American sloop of war *Peacock*, with Commodore Kennedy aboard. Mr. Edwards had been sent by the government of the United States to arrange divers commercial matters with certain powers of India, and to place the commercial establishments at the Sandwich Islands on a firm basis. But Mr. Edwards died in India, before the arrival of the *Peacock* at Honolulu, and Commodore Kennedy carried out the instructions received by Mr.

Edwards. The principal object of the mission was the construction to be given to the treaty between the United States and the Sandwich Islands. The Hawaiians and the Americans put different constructions upon this treaty; the Americans pretended that the land upon which they had erected houses had become their own property; the government of the Sandwich Islands declared, as I have just said, that the Americans and other foreigners, having built upon lands which did not belong to them, had no right to the property; that it was an act of great condescension to permit them to occupy it during their residence in the country, and that when they should leave, the State ought to resume the possession of a property, all the rights to which it had preserved. Commodore Kennedy put forth all his efforts in order to secure, by adding other Articles to the treaty, the principle contended for by his countrymen; but obstacles were thrown in his way. At the first conference, there was agreement upon every particular, and the additional articles were to be signed the next day. The next day, the government not only refused to accede to the demands of Commodore Kennedy, but it formally declared that it was decided not to permit foreigners to become landholders at the Sandwich Islands by any title whatever. Commodore Kennedy, having no specific instructions to guide him in the matter, set sail much dissatisfied, threatening the government, it is said, with the efficacious intervention of the United States.

This refusal of the government is ascribed to the

missionaries, who in my opinion have sustained, or have persuaded the government to sustain a principle, the justice of which cannot be denied. The claim to be an owner of a land, simply because an individual has built a house upon it, was not defensible even by the law of nature; but to shut the door to all accommodation in this question was altogether impolitic. It was prejudicial to the interests of the country and the people, whose welfare, and preservation even, depended on the intermingling of the nation with foreigners; for it is only in this way that these unnumbered abuses and this terrible arbitrariness under which the islanders groan can be done away, an arbitrariness and oppression become a thousand times more insupportable at present than formerly.

The Hawaiian government did wrong, in my opinion, in taking such arbitrary measures. It is certain that the erection of a house cannot give a legal claim to the land upon which the house has been built; but regard should be had to the circumstances in which the establishment was formed, to the condition of the country at the time, and then preference should be given to the actual holders. In certain cases also prescriptions should give to the holders the right of property, or it should have an influence upon the duration of the leases which the government might grant. As to the uncultivated lands, and this I believe was one of the principal objects with Commodore Kennedy, was there no legal means by which it might be brought about, that foreigners might cultivate these lands with security, and without the fear of being dispossessed, when on the point of reaping the fruits of their labors? Could not the government be induced to yield, in consideration of a certain price and for a number of years the ownership of lands which for want of laborers must remain unproductive? Could it not, while offering to purchasers every needed security, reserve to itself a pledge of sovereignty and absolute ownership, if ever it should wish to refuse to foreigners the right to become proprietors, if in short, it should wish to persevere in a system which I regard as unsustainable at the Sandwich Islands.

In conclusion, the missionaries have doubtless done good at the Sandwich Islands, but they have also done much evil in not doing all the good which it was given them to accomplish. Ought their intentions to be accused? Should credit be given to the charge of interested motives which is made against them? or should the fault be thrown back on the principles in which they themselves have been educated, on that condition attached to humanity, that no work coming from the hand of man is perfect? This question I shall not undertake to decide. My stay at the islands was not long enough to satisfy my own mind on this point, and whatever my judgment might be, I should be afraid of being unjust towards the missionaries or towards their accusers.

POSTSCRIPT

The following paragraphs appeared in The Friend, *November 15, 1850, after the last installment had appeared.*

A correspondent asks, "When will the Translations end?" We reply, with this number. Some of our readers may not have been particularly interested in these translations from a French author, but with others it has been far otherwise.

We would not wish to be understood as coinciding with all the views and opinions expressed in these articles of M. Adolphus Barrot, still, taking into consideration the fact that the writer was a Frenchman, a Catholic, a transient visitor (remaining only a few days on our shores), and furthermore, unacquainted with the native language, we are much surprised at the general correctness of his statements. He must certainly have been a good observer, and capable of winnowing wheat from chaff. Much chaff may remain, but if he had enjoyed a longer opportunity for observation, he might have cleared it away. We would merely add, that he was bound to Manila, there to act as French Consul, but has since returned to France. This article originally appeared in a publication entitled "A Review of the Two Worlds," and a copy was brought to the islands by the Rev. Mr. Richards, on his return from Europe, in 1845. We would express our obligation to the Rev. Mr. Dole for his perseverance, in thus gratuitously translating so many pages for our columns.

INDEX

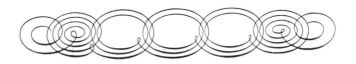